Stand-up,
Sitting Down

Jimmy Perrin

Warning:
This book contains writing of an adult nature
and is only for persons aged 18 or over.

CONTENTS

CHAPTER 1
INTRODUCTION & SMALL TALK

Holy shit balls, where do I start?

You know, when my agent instructed me to write a book about myself, my life, a kind of autobiography so to speak, I thought bring it on, piece of piss. Now I've actually sat down to start writing the thing, I haven't got anything say.

I guess the easiest way of starting is to say hello, introduce myself and tell you a little about me.

"Hello, I'm Jimmy"

That's it... No really, that's all you're getting !!

See, if you know me, you know I'm a little shy and quiet, but more importantly, I don't do talking about myself or the dreaded "Small Talk" thing – I mean what's the point?

To me small talk is just another way of someone saying, you aren't interesting enough to hold a proper conversation with, so bugger off.

"Cor, it's cold out today Jimmy, I think it might rain"

Really?

That's all you've got to say to me?

I can't tell you the amount of times I've wanted to say something back, but ended up biting my tongue.

"*Morning Jimmy, lovely day, isn't it?*"

"Yeah, so lovely in-fact that I stripped off in my garden this morning, let the sunshine tan me bollocks, then grew myself the biggest erection I've ever had"

Okay, that's never happened, but come on – If you haven't got anything interesting to say to me, a simple smile and wave would suffice.

"*Al-right Jimmy, I see the Hammers lost again on Saturday*"

Really?

"Fuck me, we must have interacting magical TV's or something, because I saw the exact same game on my TV too, but thanks for sharing that, you dick"

How about you don't tell me, wipe the smug-arse sympathetic look off your face, before you force me to respond in exactly the same way I do every time...

"Yeah I know, I'm gutted. Let's just hope we win again next week"

Yeah, like I'm that bothered by my team losing again.

Okay, off to a good start – Everyone thinks I'm rude and unapproachable now, but really, Am I? Or do I just have the nerve to walk away when people start to bore the crap out of me? I tell you what, you wouldn't find me getting the hump or wandering off, if someone walked up to me and informed me they had a really dirty dream last night.

The real Jimmy is a positive person. A person who is SO positive, that he fights off negativity with a large stick. What's more negative than someone not wanting to have a real conversation with you in passing? I'll tell you what, someone that tells you it looks like it's going to rain, holds you up for those awkward thirty seconds and makes you get caught in it anyway.

CHAPTER 2
JIMMY THE WRITER

So, who am I?

"I'm Jimmy and I'm a writer"

(I bet you couldn't guess that yourself, considering you're reading my book)

The poetically correct way of stating my profession is "Author" but I think this sucks !!

I write things down, they get printed, therefore I'm a writer.

What the fuck is an author anyway?

I'll tell you what an author is...

An author is someone that usually talks down their nose at people intelligently and says things like "Superb" or "Splendid"

They also use big fuck-off words throughout their writing to confuse readers, then sometimes even use words they don't necessarily understand themselves.

An Author is someone that takes a picture of themselves for the back of their book, usually sitting in front of their book, pulling what can only be described as a fake smile, the sour faced tits.

Oh and an author writes books, which to me is a fucking WRITER !!

I think that's one of the worst things about my job, because people relate an "Author" to highly intelligent people with huge pompous vocabulary skills.

Okay, I'll give you intelligent with me, but fuck no, I'm not pompous.

(I couldn't even spell the word pompous before looking it up)

Believe it or not, but I love writing and I love my job. To me there's nothing more special in the world than putting a smile on someone's face or making them laugh, but how can you do that being an author?

My way...

"I'm a knob, a complete dick-head"

Their way...

"I'm a convexity, an accomplished phallus head"

Doesn't really work being an author, does it? And that's why I am AND always will be, just a writer.

Some people think that being a "*Writer*" is an easy thing to be, let me tell you, it's not !!

Being a writer is one of the most punishing, unrewarding and lonely things I've ever done.

Here's a little taster of what I put myself through on a daily basis.

1- Come up with a funny idea for a book.

2- Plan that book out on paper from start to finish.

3- Spend weeks and months writing the thing, hoping it will at least make me laugh.

Sounds quite straight forward, doesn't it? Oh no, then comes what happens once you finish writing it.

1- Read it back at least five times.

2- Send it off to proof-readers, waiting for changes they demand I make.

3- Read it again, before it goes to print.

I tell you what, I normally detest my book by the time you excited readers get your hands on it. Then to top it off, I've read it so many bloody times now, that it isn't funny any more.

NOW COMES THE DREADED WAIT...

...

Waiting, worrying, waiting some more. Praying that just one person buys it and likes it.

Oh no mister writer, no time for you to worry people might think you're shit, it's onto the next book for you dear fellow.

1- Writing something new, with your confidence and concerns draining the life out of you.

2- Being ignored or laughed at by friends, because they refuse to buy your book, claiming they don't read books (The non-supportive fuck-wits)

3- Then having to juggle your new project, promote the latest book and answer questions about it.

Answer questions about it? I'm writing something new, so how the hell am I supposed to answer questions about a book I've had to drop from my head to start another one, then remember it again? You wouldn't believe how many times I've written Malcolm into a book he's not supposed to be a character in.

So, for any of you that have asked me a question about a book in the past, now you know why I always have a blank expression on my face. I'm sure some of my readers don't actually think I write the books I am promoting. I guess I can't blame them really, can I?

"Oh Jimmy, I loved the part where Malcolm and Dexter were in the taxi, drunk"

"Do you? That's great. Sorry but I have no idea what you're talking about"

Whilst you are reading Hard up 1 and talking about it, I'm currently planning out number 4 or a completely different book, so please give me a break, because I don't remember what I wrote yesterday – I'm not allowed to !!

SO, do you think a writer's life is easy now?

HA !!, Got ya - Held some back for those of you that still think it's a piece of piss.

1- Whilst writing your next book, planning out the one after that and waiting for the verdict on your latest one, its now time to get out there, do a few book signings and meet your readers.

2- Planning, writing, waiting, greeting, signing, smiling, talking about books you can't fucking remember, then comes the professional critic. The bastard that will put you down for a single full-stop out of place and label you rubbish. (Oh and whilst on the subject of the lovely critic, let me tell you a little about them)

Three of the sods laid into my first book and not one of the fuckers actually agreed on the same thing needed to improve my writing. One basically said my grammar was crap, the second said it was good, but the books format needed work - Whilst the third banged on about wonderfully descriptive linguistics, which to you and me thick fucks means, yes that word grammar again.

So here's my question to you...

"If these hot-shot critics that go around judging author's writing skills are so good at their jobs, then why don't any of the knobs agree with each-other?"

I've taught myself not to listen to critics any more, as they are (Sorry, they're) always going to criticise something you do. I know it sounds silly, but if they don't find something bad to say about you, then they wouldn't be doing their jobs properly, would they?

Saying that, who am I to criticise a critic? What the fuck do I know about grammar? I just type shit onto a computer screen after all. Hey, it's not as though I know anything about reading books, seeing as I've NEVER actually read one in my life - (Ooh another insight into who I am – The writer that doesn't read books)

What can I say? It's not as though I haven't tried, I just can't seem to take anything in. Yeah I read it, page after page, after page,

after page zzzZZZZ...

Then I simply realise I'm still on page two, haven't got a clue what's going on in the story and sit wondering why I turned page after page, after page to find myself still only on page number two.

To me books are boring. I mean, what's wrong with watching a good film instead? Yes I know, I should be careful here, after all, I make my living from you wonderful readers who take my book to bed with you.

Saying that, fuck no – Who takes a book to bed? What's wrong with having sex in bed you boring bastards?

Put my crappy book down and get your leg over. Seriously, I'm not bothered, I've been paid for your purchase anyway. Hey, as long as your bedside cabinet is stocked with tissues and you don't use my book pages to wipe up anything messy, I'm happy !!

Nope, take that back – PLEASE read my book (Yes in bed if you like) because what I guarantee my readers is, you will never know what's coming next with me. See, because of the critics that have criticised me already, I simply don't give a shit any more, so therefore will continue to write my way and do my best to...

Shock you,

Surprise you,

Frustrate you,

and sometimes even Piss you off !!

Saying that, I might get good at it one day and roll all of them together - Wow, what a book that would be !!

In the Hard Up books I've already become the first "Author" to write myself into the story.

In Heavenly I purposely left six blank pages right in the middle of the book.

In Air Hostess I turned a true story into fiction, then back into the readers true story.

Who's knows what crazy shit I will think up next? But one thing is for sure, I won't EVER write a book that is straight forward like a bloody "Author" would.

CHAPTER 3
HORSE RACING

Although I love my job as a "*Writer*" my first real love came in the form of a thoroughbred racehorse, when at aged just sixteen I was sent to a racing school to become a jockey.

Now is it just me, or does anyone else think there's something wrong with this idea? I mean, who the fuck sends a group of horny teenagers away from home for the first time in their lives and bundles them together into a hostel?

School? It was more like being on a sex education programme, gone wrong !!

I remember the teachers telling us to relax for the first few days, simply to let us settle in and acclimatise ourselves with the surroundings of our new home. Yeah, more like check out the talent on offer and pick out your mating partner for the duration of the stay. Fuck me, I don't think anyone actually got on a horse for the first week, but there was certainly plenty of riding taking place, if you know what I mean !!

Unlike most of the studs and sluts at the school, the worst thing for me was my virginity at the time. I didn't have a clue what was going on when the pairing of boy and girl took place in the TV room one night. Don't get me wrong, although I was a virgin,

I wasn't short of offers that night. It actually turned out because I was in such high demand, I got to pick the girl I wanted to pair up with, which I guess made me the biggest stud there after all.

(Hey and just think, that was me aged sixteen, weighing in at a super skinny seven stone, nothing like the sexual piece of well-built man I am today !!)

The school itself was terrible - Strict, long hours, punishing diets and sleepless nights. No, not sleepless nights because I became a stud stud, but because of the amount of students getting all kinds of home sick during the night (Usually my bloody room mate)

I think we would head down to the stable at half four in the morning, muck out (Shovel shit, for those of you that don't know horses) then ride our horses until eight. Then it was breakfast time, that saw us munching on our single dry Weetabix, before lessons started. The class would take us up to our dry piece of toast at lunchtime, then it was out on the gallops or inside the indoor school for more riding in the afternoon.

"Can I add at this point, no fucker wanted to end up in the indoor school"

It was rougher than rough !!

The indoor school meant riding a huge racehorse around in a circle on sand, without a saddle, whilst the teachers screamed and shouted to make the horse run faster. All we could do as riders is hang on for dear life and hope we didn't crash to the ground. Oh no, it's wasn't the fear of falling off a great big racehorse bombing around at forty miles an hour that we feared - It was because if you did fall off, the teacher would then kick sand in your face and you'd miss your dinner. Yes, it really was that rough at the school !!

Another thing they demanded at the school was a military standard of cleanliness inside your stable. One hair out of place on your horse, one piece of straw on the ground and you'd never hear the end of it. Saying that, now looking back, I think the pitch-fork I took around the shoulder one day was a tad FUCKING unfair !!

Don't get me wrong, the school was a massive learning experience for me and kind of turned this boy into a man (Well it taught me to run away faster anyway) If I wasn't being chased around by swinging pitch-forks, I was running from the girls all wanting a piece of my cherry pie.

Cor blimey, I can't tell you how many excuses I had to dream up, just not to have sex. Yet it seemed the more I didn't give out (Not only to my girlfriend at the time) the more everyone chased me. Strike me down if this is a lie, but even one of the student teachers came knocking at my window one night, offering herself on a plate.

"I wish she was on a plate, because I was fucking starving at this point"

I remember all my classmates geeing me on...

"Sexy twenty year old teacher Jimmy, you lucky tosser"

"The same teacher we all ogle over in class"

"The older more experienced woman sexually"

Yeah, fuck it I thought, that will help my grades !!

Okay, I didn't really think about my classroom grades at the time, but I do remember asking, why me? Yes me, a sixteen year old boy, waiting to pop my cherry, girls all over the place, a hot teacher making moves on me and the envy of all my male friends and I ask, why me? That's simply because I just wanted to be a jockey, nothing else. I didn't want different girls jumping into bed with me every night, whilst I pretended to snore and roll away from them. I didn't want girls with their new strange accents ordering me to get inside their "Keks" I just wanted to ride a fucking racehorse !!

Keks? It took me another two bloody years after the school to work out this meant knickers in Northern slang. I can't for the life of me remember what I thought she was asking me to do that night, but I didn't do it, whatever it was.

As a jockey after the school, I did manage to do pretty well for myself. I rode some very famous horses and worked for some very famous trainers, but I don't know if I actually enjoyed every single minute of the job.

Don't get me wrong, there's parts of the job that I will NEVER forget and they were actually some of the best moments of my life. For instance, being up on the gallops at five in the morning, just me and my horse. Nothing but the sound of hooves galloping faster and faster and me groaning like mad, trying to slow the sod down. It was blissful !!

Still today I get goose bumps thinking about just how beautiful and peaceful it was out there.

BUT THEN CAME THE SHITTY PARTS OF THE JOB...

Mucking out? Bollocks, let the dirty bastard clean up it's own shit.

Grooming? Fuck that, I didn't even groom myself properly back then.

The diet? Give me the biggest, greasiest cheese burger I've ever had, before I start mugging the horse, who seemed to eat better than the us anyway.

Ten hours and thirty minutes of my twelve hour day, I just stuck my head down and got on with the horrid duties of the job. Only the hour and a half on the gallops in the morning, made it all worth while, so that tells you just how beautiful it really was on those gallops !!

That's why when I first started out as a stable lad, I told people I was already a jockey. Not because I had ideas above my station, not because I'd already been promoted in secret, simply because I wasn't a stable lad... I mean, I was a stable lad at the beginning, but I wasn't, if you know what I mean?

Okay then, I didn't consider myself a stable lad, because I was shit at it. Back breaking mucking out? Fine, done it. Wheel the wheelbarrow right to the end of the track (A mile away) and empty it? Fuck no !!

What I used to do is make my stable all sparkly and clean, then go next door to someone else's stable and empty my wheelbarrow in there.

What? Don't judge me, who was going to find out? Hey, it's not like the horse was going to tell it's groom and grass me up, was it? It's not as though all horse shit doesn't look the same?

I pretty much did things like this throughout my apprenticeship, but didn't feel bad about it. See, whilst everyone else enjoyed the stable side of the job and looking after the horses, I just wanted to get out there and jump those Grand National fences.

Nowadays when people find out I was a (Stable lad / Jockey) they ask me why I gave it up, then strangely take guesses at the reason I don't ride any more.

"*Was it you got too fat and couldn't do the diet thing?*"

"*Yes the dieting for a jockey was shit and did play some part, but no I didn't get too fat, you cheeky bastard*"

"*Did you have a serious fall from a horse and you were forced to give up?*"

"*Yes I had some really dodgy tumbles, but no, that wasn't the reason either*"

"*Was it the strict military style operation?*"

"*Yes, that pissed me off most of the time, but again, not the whole reason I left the job*"

Go on then, ask the one you're thinking...

"*Did I get caught dumping my wheelbarrow in someone else's stable?*"

"*Nope, not that either*"

If I'm honest, it's just a really tough life and one where, if your face fits, you'll do well. Seeing as my skull cap (helmet) wouldn't even fit over my head properly, my face never seemed to fit and there was always someone on my back. If it wasn't girls trying to bed me, it was their angry boyfriends hating me. If it wasn't angry boyfriends hating me, it was angry bosses telling me to work faster.

You try working faster, dieting on a single grape a day, work twelve hour shifts, using all your energy to control a ton and a half of horse, then tell me you wouldn't find it hard.

Saying that, there was one part of the job, I hated most of all. One part of the job that not only pissed me off, but confused the hell out of me on a daily basis – That was feeding time !!

This is probably one of the most important parts of training a racehorse, more important than getting it fit enough to race. If those horses don't eat a certain meal, it could hamper not only their well-being, but their chances of winning a racecourse event.

Now, is it just me, or would anyone else have this same problem? Because lets face it right now – This was my BIGGEST nightmare at the stables.

"Can anyone else tell the difference between two horses?"

No, I'm not talking about a grey one, a brown one and a chestnut, I'm talking line fifty brown one's in a row, side-by-side in their stables and know which one is which.

This was the part of the job I hated most !!

The trainer would make up all the strict bowls of food, then hand them out one by one to staff ready to feed. Nightmare !!

No names on stable doors, no numbers, no anything. Just a quick,

"Dicey"

"Lady Shadow"

"Willersford"

Then off you go with your bowl. It seemed everyone else but me would walk straight over to the horse in question and give over it's food. Me? I fucking guessed !!

"Willersford, Willersford, you don't look like a Willersford, oh here you are"

I didn't have a clue !!

How could they walk over to one of fifty horses and know which one it was? How the hell was I supposed to find my horse every single evening? I've heard of being dyslectic when reading or writing, but I really thought I had the same problem when I came down to identifying a horse by name.

There's little me, probably giving the wrong horse the wrong dinner, praying that it will eat it as quickly as possible, so no-one would see. (Hey, I guess that's why our stable never had any winners whilst I worked there !!)

Oh no, it didn't just stop at feeding, this happened all over the place.

"Hey Jimmy, go and fetch Athlete from the field and take him to the stables"

"Jimmy, tack-up Garrison and work-ride out on the gallops"

"Athlete? Garrison? I guess you mean the first fucking horse I come to then"

Okay, I never got caught feeding the wrong horse, but this whole name thing did manage to backfire on me once.

<u>Here's the story</u>

I was late for work one morning and had missed my first ride on the gallops (This is only two days in with a new stable and new horses, by the way) The boss is already pissed at me and tells me to get Flyns tacked-up and out onto gallop number two for a steady mile canter. I'm more than happy with the command, but explain I don't know where gallop number two is, be it my first time out in the area.

*"**FIND IT !!**"*

I find Flyns easy enough, tack her up and head out nervously onto the country roads of Berkshire for the first time in my life. Lucky for me I pass somebody I was at racing school with (Who rode for a different trainer) and he pointed me in the right direction.

Lucky really, because if he'd have thought about it, he could have repaid me for all the practical jokes I once played on him at the school.

Perfect day, ***perfect*** ride, ***perfect*** exercise of my horse !!

That's until of course I got back to the stables and I'm told that I took out the wrong horse. Fuck me, it's brown, it has four legs, bastard even nodded it's head when I walked over and asked if it was Flyns or not that morning.

Turns out my real, honest, more embarrassing downfall during my racing career, was simply because I couldn't tell one horse from the next. No, I never got sacked for it, but always felt I was on borrowed time. The only positive I take from this whole experience now is – I still love horse racing today and enjoy watching it on the TV. Then I enjoy it even more, when I here the commentator utter these very common words...

"This horse won't be winning today, the stable is badly out of form"

With these words I take comfort, because I know somehow, some way, somewhere out there, there's another little me exercising and feeding the wrong fucking horse.

CHAPTER 4
SCHOOL & TEACHING

As you can tell, I had an up and down time during my racing career and more downs than up's during my time at the school. But believe it or not, this was in-fact the best school I'd ever attended, as primary / secondary school sucked even more !!

Without going into too much detail, I was bullied throughout my school life and teased for being very small. This bullying not only had an effect on my confidence, but my school work too and I suffered big time because of it.

Now don't be going all soft on me, don't be sitting there feeling sorry for me. Later in the book I will tell you how I turned all of this into a positive, so shove your sympathy up your bum !!

When I say I suffered at school, I really did. My progress fell through the floor so much that by the end of primary school, I still couldn't read, write or spell and had to have teachers miss their lunch to read with me. When I say read with me, I mean by the teacher forcing me to read and bellowing at me if I couldn't do it.

*"**Come on James, the word is it. How can you not pronounce this word?**"*

Okay, it wasn't as bad as that particular word, but I definitely struggled with words like, say, day and way. Now I know the old story about school's these days getting softer and softer. And I know that my dad had it worse than me and my Granddad before him, but really? How the fuck is a child meant to grow in confidence, if all the teacher is going to do is scream at him? (Whilst may I add, spitting the banana from her packed lunch all over me)

Oh no, that wasn't the worse part.

It got even worse, because after she'd told me the word for the third time and I still didn't get it right, she would then place her hands on my shoulders and shake the shit out of me, whilst continuing to scream banana bits in my face.

"HoW cAn I SAY tHe worD, If you're shaKINg ME ArOund?"

Nope, I never cried this either, but wow, what a difference in school's today. Old Mrs Steward would be locked up for just breathing banana breath over me, let alone giving me her impression of an aggressive tight gripped tumble dryer.

"Oh, the good old days"

If I wasn't being mocked for my height or beaten up in the playground, the teachers were looking after me in their own very special way !!

Lucky for me, there was just one teacher throughout my school life who did have patience with little me and she, lets call her Mrs Watkins, gave me confidence beyond belief.

I'm not sure why this one teacher decided to adore me, but it really was the difference between me hating school completely and hating it a little less.

Saying this, I can't honestly confess I appreciated the attention as a child, I mean, who really wants an overly nice teacher mollycoddling them at that age? Fuck, that was all I needed - "Teachers Pet" added to the list of shitty things the bullies would throw my way.

It wasn't until I'd left school and finished with the horses, that this lovely lady realised I was looking for a new job and offered me one (Well, an interview for one) Oh did I forget to mention, she was now by this time in the head teachers office and running the school? Hey, who else would have been good enough over the years to get promoted? A teacher with a huge heart and compassion for her pupils? Or Mrs Shake-the-shit out of the kids Steward?

I honestly don't remember what was more surreal that day. Heading back to primary school after so many years? Or sitting in a committee interview with my old teacher asking the questions? That day for me was like the weirdest trip I have ever been on.

First the school seemed a lot smaller than I remembered. I mean, It wasn't like it had shrunk or anything, because I knew that was impossible, but I also knew I hadn't fucking grown any since leaving there, so it had to be something. It was also the strangest feeling in the world being able to walk into the staff room. You know, that room which for so many years was completely forbidden to enter for us kids. I remember being inside looking out at all the children walking past and thinking...

"That's it you little shit-bag, just keep walking, no kids allowed in here"

Granted it shouldn't have been one of the first things I thought starting in a new job with children, but it's as though I was now one of them, remembering how all the staff treated us years ago.

Anyway, I was given my job title after sailing through the interview (I say sailed through, but I don't actually think I said a word before being congratulated)

The job title was "*PE development officer*"

What was my first thought? "*PE development, what now?*"

Turns out I was going to design the schools sporting events for the term and run them with a small team behind me (Small team being two other staff members)

How?

I'm going to be paid to do what?

Well strap one on and fuck me up the arse !!

Can you believe it, me in charge of PE? Me setting out the sports programme and running it?

To cut a long story short, I wasn't really any good at this job either. I mean, fancy giving me a football, a load of small children and a playground to run around in.

I think my professionalism only lasted a few days, then I was getting stuck-in and if I'm honest, enjoying what once was a horrid time for me in that playground. Because now instead of playing football, being bullied, I was now one of the BIGGER kids !!

(Weird being in the staffroom, weird calling my old teacher by her first name, then even weirder when all the kids seemed to love me and I became the favourite staff member at the school)

How could I be admired like this? All I was doing is playing football. Yes I know, there should have been more sports on offer in my term programme. Rugby, bench-ball, netball, rounders and hockey, they were all in my plans, but it was football... Football where I was the best player, the fastest and the top scorer may I add.

I loved being at the school and I love the responsibility the job taught me, but the weirdest thing that happened, was me getting involved with another teacher. I think that was the craziest shit that happened, because although I was teaching myself, I still felt like a child in the playground. Then when this more professional, grown-up woman showed an interest in me, it just felt so fucking strange !!

I remember her offering me a lift home after school one day and it was like...

"I shouldn't really be getting into a car with a stranger"

I then remember our first kiss and I felt like...

"Thank you Miss... Here's an apple"

Needless to say the relationship didn't blossom, but we are still friends today, so I guess I made some kind of impact !!

By this stage of my life, well a year or so beforehand (Aged seventeen to be exact) I was a virgin no more and finally gave my cherry away. I'm not sure why I left it until this age, but I guess after the racing school, I was still trying to find out what the fuck "Keks" were in my sex eduction booklet.

Losing my virginity was probably one of the most daunting

experiences of my life. Not only was the girl I chose more experienced than me, but she was one of these girls that are, shall we say, fast in bed. (When I say fast in bed, I mean - In, out, shake it all about) Nope, zero foreplay, zero touching, not even an attempt to do the Hokey Cokey... It was a simple case of,

"Wham-bam-thanku-mam"

Faster than it's taken to type it all out in-fact !!

Whilst I tried to cope with the grip of my first time condom and after only about sixty seconds, she had finished. If that wasn't bad enough and the pressure to do my business wasn't getting harder, the bitch then starting humming a tune. There's little me trying to give her all my inexperienced best moves, whilst praying what I was doing was good enough and there's her, getting herself into a Meat Loaf classic. Needless to say, I didn't go back there again.

"No, I just left the condom off for the next year or so and had my own little race to finish before her"

CHAPTER 5
REDCOAT

Once my contract ended at the school and my former teacher and now friend informed me they couldn't afford to keep me on, I turned my attention to something I never thought I would do.

I wanted to become a holiday rep at Butlins and wear one of those famous red jackets. Again, I have no idea how little shy me beat over two thousand applicants to the job, but I did it and moved down to Bognor Regis.

Stranger than the horses I couldn't identify, stranger than the teaching job I never actually taught anything doing - This was the strangest job to walk into ever !!

Living on a holiday camp site twenty-four hours a day...

Having as much fun as possible, then sharing that fun with holiday-makers...

Being paid to be happy all day, then dance in nightclubs throughout the night...

Nothing could really touch how excited I was !!

Turns out life as a Butlins redcoat was in-fact a lot tougher than being a jockey or teacher.

Here's how my day panned out on a daily basis

8am, down to the office to be briefed on today's duties.

9am, setting up those said duties (Which could have been anything from running the go-cart track, running the kids club, to competitions or hosting on stage)

That took us up to lunch-time, where we had an hour break.

2pm, afternoon activity, before dinner at five, then a quick change of uniform.

5pm, feature in today's evening performance (Which could have been singing on stage, acting or hosting the karaoke bar)

And that took us right through til midnight, where we signed off as redcoats. You know, they say the job of a redcoat is only for the young? It isn't - It's for those fuckers with enough stamina to work a sixteen hour day !!

Oh no, It didn't stop there, because come midnight you needed time to unwind, needed time for a few drinks in the staff bar with your friends.

You try getting up at seven every morning (Usually hung-over) Then dragging your arse back to your chalet dunk at four every morning – It was fucking exhausting !!

OH NO, BUT IT DIDN'T STOP THERE EITHER !!

After about every two weeks, you were called into the office for an appraisal. This little meeting could actually see you sacked and sent home if you weren't doing your job well enough. Although I passed every one of my appraisals, they seemed to tell everyone the same thing...

"*You work for Butlins*"

"*Butlins means you walk around with a smile on your face twenty-four hours a day*"

"*Anyone not smiling, will be sacked*"

Fair enough, right? It was a holiday camp after all.

But you try holding that same fucking smile on your face, when you haven't slept in weeks, then you've got a pile of uniforms to wash and iron in the little time you get to rest, It's not easy !!

Oh no, but it didn't stop there, once again !!

In the few hours off work during the day, you then have to sift through loads of fan-mail coming in from holiday-makers past and present. See, the redcoat that received the most mail and responded, became top redcoat and guaranteed there place in the job next season.

SO, not only were the days and nights long, but then all the redcoats started competing for this top spot, hall of fame, crappy redcoat title and counting their bloody mail.

Guess who won it?

Guess who was the best redcoat there?

Yes, this dick-head, yours bloody truly !!

Why did I have to do my job so well?

Why did the bastard holiday-makers like me most?

Happy, smiling faces? I wanted to kill the fuckers !!

I blamed it and still do today, on my magical dancing skills - I totally rocked the Y.M.C.A routine !!

Oh no, but It... didn't... stop.... there.

I think the breaking point for me came when I was putting in those long hours, starting to look like crap in the hundreds of pictures I posed for and spent all my free time writing letters to fans. It actually broke me so bad, that I wasn't staying in the clubs past midnight any more. Oh no, I wasn't going home to sleep, I was then sleeping with all the holiday-makers throwing there chalet keys at me.

It wasn't bad at first, because sex with one woman didn't last longer than the hours of drinking I was doing beforehand, but when it reached two or three women every night, not even I could keep it up for long. (I mean keep up the grueling schedule, not my performance in the bedroom, you understand?)

So that was it, another career fucked and down the toilet, then me feeling by the end of it that I had almost been doubly fucked, career wise and to death by those LUCKY holiday-makers !!

CHAPTER 6
HOSPITAL

Apart from spending seven years as a bingo caller, I also had a tiny stint in nursing. I say tiny stint in nursing, because once again I had no idea what I was doing and absolutely no idea how the fuck I got the job.

Throughout my life all I've really enjoyed doing is helping people and making them smile, so when I saw this job advertised for a HCA at the local hospital, I jumped at it. I didn't think I'd get it, but once I knew I was getting interviewed by two women, I knew one of my cheeky smiles and a little bit of subtle seduction would work wonders.

Fuck me, it did, what a surprise !!

Then came the shock...

"What the fuck am I going to the hospital for?"

"What the fuck do I know about medical shit?"

Turns out, I didn't need to know anything, as for the first few days in the job, I just winged the whole thing and seemed to do it right.

I mean, learning to spell words like colonoscopy and endoscopy was difficult, but it was even more difficult learning what the bastard words actually meant as I wrote them down.

I would at this point give you a whole list of medical words I had to learn to spell, but seeing as I can't fucking spell them again now (Let alone, remember them) I can't !!

My job was simply – Do anything the nurses couldn't be bothered to do themselves, which simply meant, drink coffee !!

That seemed to be what they enjoyed doing most, so who was I to say no when offered a cup?

Two weeks into the job I was doing so well at drinking coffee, that I was promoted from "HCA" to "Patient co-ordinator" Yeah, me a patient co-ordinator – Who see that coming?

<u>The conversation went a little like this</u>

"***Jimmy, can I have a word***"

"*Sure*"

"***You're doing such a great job here, that we want to offer you a new post***"

"*Okay*"

"***It's as patient co-ordinator. Are you interested?***"

"*Sure*"

Man of many fucking words me !!

No-one actually told me what the bloody job was. Saying that, why the fuck did I accept a job, when I didn't know what it was?

What if it meant working in the mortuary?

What if it meant dealing with a dreaded needle?

Patient co-ordinator? What if it meant co-ordinating with patients and having the fucking operation done myself for them?

It turns out because I was so good around people, they thought it would be a good idea to have me meet and greet patients as they got ready for an operation. (Basically settle them down, offer one of my smiles and help them relax)

Relax?

Me in a hospital, around needles and they want ME to relax people? That's like shoving a load of ice-cubes down my pants and telling me to stand still !!

My job was to travel up and down Northern Scotland with a team of pre-op nurses and co-ordinate pre-op clinics. Get all that?

Another two weeks down the line, my duties were added too again and I was pulling patients medical records and getting them ready for the operating theatre too.

Now, I don't really know how hard it should be to match someone's name to a file and pull it out of the cabinet, or ring a hospital, then chase up someone's file, but I apparently did this really well too. So well in-fact that I wasn't just visiting clinics any more, but I was given my own little office and told to re-design the medical records department.

No longer was I worried about not being able to do the job there at the hospital. No, not because I knew what I was doing, but because I had this little office to hide away in.

Clinics, visiting patients on the ward, hiding away in my new medical records office and still drinking coffee with the nurses. I wasn't exactly sure what my job at the hospital was any more, but everyone seemed to love me and I worked really hard when I knew what it was I was doing.

That's until my boss left the hospital and a new one came in to take over. What a fat fucking knob-head he was. I mean, such a big knob-head, the fucker probably didn't have one between his legs to compensate !!

All this arsehole did was sit in his office, eat bags and bags of crisps and send out orders by memo to staff. Don't get me wrong, he wasn't a complete knob-head all the time, sometimes he was a huge fanny-fuck face too !!

So why did I hate him so much?

Because whilst I was working my butt off doing two jobs at the same time, he was still sitting there throwing another pack of prawn **COCK** tail **DOWN HIS THROAT**.

Whilst every single staff member appreciated how hard I worked, how much I cheered the place up, the COCK went and got all jealous on me. Ahhhhh, poor new boss man feeling threatened by little me - Poor new boss man wanted to be laughed with and respected as much as I was.

He fucking hated me, didn't he?

Tit should have put his crisp down, got off his fat backside and helped out then, shouldn't he?

ANYWAY, seems after all I've said and felt about him, I got him wrong, because there he was coming out of his office to notice my hard work, then promote me again.

YES PROMOTE ME !!

Here's how the conversation went.

"Jimmy, are you out on clinic today or working in medical records?"

"I'm doing a little both Mr boss man Sir... Mr Slim, toned and such a great person Sir"

Okay, you know I didn't say this...

"Records this morning and clinic this afternoon"

"No, you're not"

"What in-fact you are doing is whatever I tell you to do"

"What in-fat arse, what?"

Yeah, didn't say this either, but thought it.

"There's some shelves I need putting up in my office, get onto it Jimmy lad"

(Oh and can I say, this was done in front of all my nurse friends to belittle me)

Me being me, nodded my head, smiled, then set about building them as requested. (Yeah, In hope they would fall off the wall and squish the fat fucker thin)

It wasn't until I was having ANOTHER coffee with the nurses an hour later, that they couldn't believe how he spoke to me and what he ordered me to do.

"Jimmy you work the clinics, you're not a janitor. You should have told him where to get off"

"What like you did standing there, pissing your knickers?"

(Nope, didn't say this again)

Yes I built the shelves, but that even backfired on me.

Why did I have to have so much fun doing it?

Why did the staff have to keep coming in the room to see me?

"Well done Jimmy, great job"

Yes, this came from Mr Fat fuck himself.

Just before...

"Tomorrow, we'll have a talk about your job here and your new duties"

That night I couldn't imagine what he could possibly add to the two jobs I was already doing, but when I walked in the next day, I did.

"There's me the manager, the surgeons, the nurses. Then comes the admin staff, the porters and finally you Jimmy"

Okay, I didn't expect to be at the top of the list, but I didn't think I would be bottom either, I was running the medical records department, if you didn't already know.

"Jimmy, I'm taking you out of medical records (I used to run medical records) *and cutting your clinic visits"*

PLEASE DON'T SAY I'M THE JANITOR,

PLEASE DON'T SAY JANITOR !!

"Your official title right now is dogs body and you answer to everyone"

PLEASE SAY JANITOR, PLEASE SAY JANITOR !!

Wow, I don't think I've ever had anyone feel so threatened by me, that they'd stoop so low. (Not that the fat fuck could stoop low, being the bouncy castle he was)

THAT WAS IT !!

You know, I can take all kinds of shit, even be mocked or laughed at, but there's only so far you can push me and this Jabba-the-hut mother fucker just pressed all my buttons. I basically gave him what for and told him I was taking the rest of the day off.

"Walk out Jimmy and I will be forced to sack you"

"Don't force the issue fatty, because you won't make me quit"

Ironically, he then asked if I just insulted him (Yeah right after the dogs body comment) then threatened to sack me for this now. Oh good, just where I need you, lard-arse !!

See I knew people liked me, I knew some of the staff would back me up and I planned to rip the shit out of him at a tribunal. Oops, even this backfired. I mean, how the hell was I suppose to know all my so-called friends would turn their back on me?

How was I supposed to know they valued their jobs more than our friendship?

It was a lonely walk through the hospital when I turned up for my meeting, especially when those so-called friends then stood there giving me daggers, but I didn't back down. (Told you, once my button is pressed, it stays fucking pressed)

In the end I got my job back, then simply told them where to shove it, but fuck do I hate bullies !!

CHAPTER 7
THE BULLY

Bullies really are the scum of the earth in my eyes. Really, give me a bank robber any day of the week. I mean, what's Mr Bank-jobs problem? His problem? Simple, he needs the money.

What reason is there to be a bully?

What kind of pleasure can one person gain hurting someone else?

I'm not sure why I feel like this. Maybe it's the fact I had it throughout my school life, or maybe it's... Nope, there's no reason – I just can't stand the pricks !!

I've dealt with so many bullies over the years, since making a stand after leaving school - I've fought them, I've chased them off, I've even humiliated the scum-bags.

Bullies come in all different shapes and sizes, ranging from control freaks, dictators, to mentality abusive people and those guys that walk around playing the hard man.

I CAN'T STAND ANY OF THEM !!

Although Jabba-the-hut at the hospital was a dictator, that got off belittling people, then using his power and position to fuck them over, I fucked him in the end and he's just one in a long line of people I have taken down.

Don't get me wrong – I hate violence with a passion.

I believe that life is too short to waste it fighting, but if as I said my buttons are pushed, fuck will I fight !!

I think my favourite kind of bully is the hard man one, the one that threatens to kill you for smiling at him the wrong way.

"I smiled at you wrong? Really? Don't you know I worked at Butlins for ages and this smirk on my face is now a permanent disfigurement, you insulting cruel bastard?"

I mean, why walk around with a huge chip on your shoulder, thinking you're better than everyone else? Hasn't he grown-up yet? Does he really think there's no-one better in the world than him?

"I'm a writer yeah? There are better writers out there than me"

"I've got a pretty good body – There are better bodies out there than mine"

"I'm a sex machine in the bedroom"

Okay, maybe this one shouldn't be used as an example, because I am pretty damn good... My point is - I may be confident, I may come across as cocky, but I am also down to earth and certainly don't walk around with a chip on my shoulder or get off on bullying people.

I think the worst bully I ever come across was an arrogant wanker, who thought the world owed him something.

He pushed my buttons all the bloody time !!

"Look at me walking down the street thinking I'm the dogs bollocks"

"Look at my flash car, all shiny and shit"

"If you look at me or my woman in the wrong way, I will beat you up, because I can"

"You got a problem little Jimmy? Do you think you're man enough to take me on?"

"My bitch is controlled and owned by me. I'll fuck anyone up who looks at her"

MM-mm, OKAY THEN !!

I Can't tell you how many times I had to listen to the same rubbish come out of his mouth, but in the end he broke me and I taught myself how to deal with people like this.

"You smiling at me Jimmy?"

"You got something to smile about?"

"Want me to wipe that smile off your face?"

I just stood there, made my smile wider and told him I didn't want to fight him.

"Yeah, of course you don't. Why would you want to take a beating?"

"Do you know how much I would hurt you?"

"Are you sure I can't tempt you to try it?"

Once again, I thanked him for his aggressive manner, but told him I didn't want to fight.

Now, you'd think he'd have got the message after the second time of asking me, but he didn't. Instead as soon as his girlfriend came out of the house, he started again and this time, he was even more bullish about it.

"You looking at my bitch Jimmy?"

"Hey bitch, do you fancy a little bit of Jimmy, or a real man like me?"

For the third and FINAL time I told him, I didn't want to fight, then basically told him I didn't like violence and that I was a lover not a fighter.

"Lover not a fighter? That's something only a pussy would say"

"You're a bigger pussy than my bitch"

"Come on Jimmy, I'll even let you hit me first. Come on, just say the word"

Wow, turns out the third and final time, wasn't in-fact the final time, was it?

"Go on Jimmy, walk away, be the pussy I think you are"

"It's not like you would have won anyway"

"Come on, say it, say what's on your mind, so I can beat you"

Should I? Should I say something?

Did I really need to have this fight?

Oh yeah, I opened my mouth al-right, but not in the way he thought I would. I just stayed calm, smiled a bit wider, then dared myself to say it.

"Come on Jimmy, I know you want to say something"

"Say it you pussy, make me angry"

"Nothing you can say will bother me, before I batter you"

"OKAY THEN, I FUCKED YOUR GIRLFRIEND LAST NIGHT"

Wow, all that build up, all those threatening words and I shut him up with one sentence (It was a bit of an anti-climax really)

Did I need to fight?

Did I really need to sit him on his backside like I knew I could?

No, the fight was already over !!

I don't do bullying of any kind and although I should always stay out of the way or tell myself it's none of my business, I always end up getting myself involved.

(Why the fuck does anyone want to ruin someone else's life?)

I guess what you're asking now is, did I really have sex with his girlfriend? I mean, I could have just said it to shut him up, couldn't I? Well that's not for me to say, but what I will tell you is – She thanked me, she left him, she moved away and she got herself happy because I helped her.

Oh go on then – Yeah I did, all night long, but I never made a habit of doing it this way.

I know it's not the same thing, but another kind of person I can't stand is fake two-faced people.

People with money, people that think they are better than everyone else, based on their lavish lifestyle. (Yeah, lavish upper classed lifestyles, but not having as much fun in life as me)

Although I have experienced this all my life too, I think the best example of it happening recently, was when I was down at Earls Court promoting "Hard Up 1"

There's down to earth me wandering around the place, feeling out of place and slightly under-dressed, then there's a group of them standing around, talking about my book.

"Oh no, one thinks this author uses far too much dialogue in his writing"

This happened whilst she had her back to me and I just stood there listening. Suddenly it was one of those moments where one of her friends spotted me and tried to let her know I was there, without actually saying it. She turned round with a big fake smile on her face and looked me, the under-dressed scum-bag up and down.

"Tremendous book young man, you are a very talented writer"

UP YOUR BUM BITCH,

I JUST HEARD WHAT YOU SAID !!

(Again, I only thought this)

Instead, I just stood there and said a shy thank you, with another big smile.

So when did she press my button? Where did I draw the line?

…

"**Come on young man, talk to me, tell me about your books. You won't get anywhere in this industry without learning to open your mouth**"

Patronizing bitch !!

This was said at the same time she turned to her posh friends, laughed at me, told them I'm just an amateur writer, then turned back and demand I speak to her again.

"I WOULD LOVE, BUT I STUPIDLY USED ALL MY DIALOGUE IN MY WRITING"

With that, I gave her a little wink, looked her up and down with a disgusted look on MY face, then skipped away all happy again.

Her face was a picture. Good, the two-faced bitch !!

Number one rule with me – Say it how it is !!

I would rather someone hate my writing, than pretend to like it. There's nothing worse in the world than a two-faced back-stabber, being nice to your face, then slagging you off behind it.

Read one of my books, I will appreciate it.

Enjoy one of my books, I will want you to read more.

Love what I do, I will literally take you on the journey with me.

Talk about me behind my back – I won't like you very much and you will get things like the following.

....

"Who the fuck does she think she is? Miss married into money, looking down her ski-sloped nose at me"

"Looking at me like I was a piece of shit, yet wearing a fucking perfume that clearly smells like the stuff"

"Looking at me like I'm a piece of rough. Yeah the piece of rough people like her fantasize about, because they're too fucking prudish to have a sex life"

"Probably feels that doing it doggy-style is beneath her, because it just sounds too vulgar, yet not realising her husband is banging his secretary like this every day"

Shall I stop? Shall I fuck !!

"Goes and buys her gold tinned biscuits on Oxford Street, because normal supermarkets are too common, yet not having the mentality to realise they come from the same fucking factory"

"Is probably going straight onto the opera after Earls Court, because that's what posh people do. Yet will secretly sit there wetting herself over the leotard bulge on stage, because she's too stuck-up to use porn"

"She probably drinks in wine bars instead of pubs. That's just in-case she has a few too many drinks, then completely embarrasses herself by having fun"

"She's the kind of person that says she's too busy to watch TV, claiming it's fake. Yet she's far too busy booking her next face-lift or boob job on hubbies credit card, which to me is neither watch-able, real or entertaining"

One more...

"Did you see the big fuck-off diamond ring on her finger? That just says to me that she's overcompensating for the other rings on her being, not being used enough"

Now I know some of you reading this might think I am over-stepping the mark here or being a little too hard on her, but why? It's not like I said any of this shit, is it? I wasn't the one telling someone I enjoyed a book, just before telling friends I didn't.

Fake two-faced people and bullies, I can't stand them !!

Saying that, there is just one more type of person that winds me up too. (Yes, just one more)

Magicians !!

No, not those people that perform on stage and pull rabbits out of hats. I'm talking about the people that don't seem to work, then magically the work is done.

<u>Take the builder for instance</u>

All you see walking past a building site everyday is a pile of rubble, then those guys either standing around chatting to each-other or bending over with their huge "Builders Bums" on show. It really doesn't matter how many times you see them, there they are seemingly not doing what they're paid to do.

So where does the magic come from?

Well, where the fuck did that house spring up from?

One minute it's a work site, then there's a fucking house !!

Who's actually doing it? I was watching them all the time.

Are they like the tooth-fairy that do their work at night?

Okay, I can't say it bothers me or I class these "Hard workers" in the same light as a bully or fake, but they bully my brain with all their head-fucking invisible work.

<u>Another one? How about the lap dancer then?</u>

Yes, I've been to a few, but only because my friends dragged me inside, you understand. And when I say dragged me inside, I mean kicking and screaming because I am so against it and find the whole thing completely degrading to women.

<u>I think the last time, the conversation went something like this</u>

"*Jimmy, do you see what kind of club is next door to the one we are in?*"

"Yeah"

"*Do you...??*"

"Let's go"

Hey, there's no need to ask me something twice. Saying that, I don't think a "Do you" merits once, let alone twice, does it?

Anyway, the magic of the lap dancer...

To be perfectly honest I don't have a problem drinking in a place like this, but I draw the line when half-naked women start approaching you for a private dance, then bug the crap out of you all night long for it.

"Hello sexy, do you want me to dance for you in private?"

Okay, this bits not too bad. I mean, who doesn't like being called sexy or offered a private dance? It's when you say "Oh al-right" then suddenly it's all about the fee.

Why the fuck do they have to ruin a perfectly nice chat?

Why if they like dancing so much, do they feel they need to talk money?

How the fuck do they manage to take a man into one of those little booths, flash some flesh, gyrate a few body parts at him, then make him want to pay even more for a second dance? It's that bad, that I've even seen a man come out and claim the dancer actually fancied him. (Yeah, she fancied you so much, that she fleeced your wallet, you tit)

How do they do it?

Every dude in there hates the idea of parting with his cash before he goes in, yet they always seem to drag themselves away with an empty wallet or feeling loved by one of the girls.

Me? I guess I'm different.

Whilst I sit there knowing she's just performed the same dance on the guy before successfully, I don't let that success go to her head. Hey, there's nothing like keeping people level headed, grounded or on their toes.

I can see it in their eyes whilst they dance for me.

"Hey, the guy before was panting heavily at this point, why aren't you?"

It's only when I see the "He must be gay" in their eyes, that I then give a little of that success back.

I guess what it comes down to is, I can't really be teased or seduced, or would rather be the one doing the teasing, lap dancer or not. Don't get me wrong, I pay up, I thank them, I even tell them they did well, but I make them work for it and tease them a little first.

Hey, if I was to be horrible to a dancer, I'd be completely honest...

"*Hey baby, do you fancy a private dance?*"

"*Yeah okay then, but it will cost you twenty quid to dance for me*"

OR better still...

"*How about I pay you, we go back there and I dance for you?*"

Yeah, that's more me - All about the giving, not the taking !!

Before anyone thinks I'm weird or that I spend my time in lap dancing clubs - Can I just confess I've only ever been inside three before and I can't see myself going in one again. (Well, that's unless my friends drag me in kicking and screaming once more)

I think the final kind of people that amaze me with their head-fucking magical skills, are the politicians.

(Fuck, they speak some crap, don't they?)

Don't they realise to us normal people, they just look like a bunch of jumped up private-school nerds, who have swallowed the polite version of the dictionary? Me? I'd much rather watch Westminster on TV, with some real people on the screen.

"*Can you tell me why you won't deal with the policy's you've promised the people of the UK?*"

Yawn, Yawn, boring Yawn !!

"*No I can't you fucking tit-head, now leave me alone*"

So much more honest, so much more watch-able !!

So where's the magic?

How the fuck do these private-school knob-heads speak so much shit over the years, break every promise made, yet keep getting voted into power? Am I missing something? Was there a TV programme I missed, where these people actually grew a personality? Are the people of the UK really seeing something I can't see?

It really doesn't matter what they say, it just sounds so shit !!

CHAPTER 8
THE CHANGING WORLD

Take the governments view on teenage pregnancy for instance...

"What we're going to do is better sex eduction classes at school and hand out more and more free condoms to cut the pregnancy overload"

ER... How about stop teaching them to have sex so young, you pricks !!

Now, I haven't got a personal issue with the age of consent (So to speak) but come on, it can be handled so much better than the way it's done today.

<u>The way it stands at the moment</u>

1 – Sex education at school aged around ten.

2 – Taught about the birds and the bees, then where babies come from.

3 – Handed condoms at sixteen.

<u>How about doing it my way</u>

Leave sex education until they are sixteen. I say this because I find it really strange that you would educate it all at such a young age, then demand they wait for another five or six years before doing it all themselves.

What's the point?

You wouldn't get a woman pole-dancing in front of a child, all sexy and shit, then telling them they've got to wait until they are eighteen to see the full nude version, so why are we teaching children this stuff so early?

Once they are sixteen, I propose instead of handing out condoms and demanding they not rush doing it, I would hand over a sex toy. Bear with me, I know it sounds strange, but just think about it.

The way now

Sex education at ten, handed condoms at fifteen and sixteen, then told not to rush. Teenage pregnancy on the up, sexually transmitted diseases taking over the world.

My way

Show sixteen year old girls how to use a toy, then inform her she's not allowed near a boy until she's experienced enough. Then and only then, can you hand over those condoms.

Hey, why not? Pilots have to have a certain amount of flying experience before they can fly passengers, so why can't a girl use a toy, instead of the real thing, then grow in confidence and experience first?

I mean really, how many of us end up having an amazing first time experience anyway? (We all know I didn't) If the girl can learn about herself first and what it's all about, surely this would stop youngsters rushing to get their leg over and cut teenage pregnancy.

I can't really say I am into politics or follow it, but I find it fascinating just how much they bull-shit their way through a day and get it wrong.

Take another example...

How is it the age of consent is sixteen, yet you can't watch or purchase pornography until you're eighteen?

Surely watching it instead of doing it, cuts teenage pregnancy?

Surely watching is educational?

How the fuck is a sixteen year old allowed to ride one in real life, yet can't watch?

Saying that and going back to my sex toy proposal - How can a sixteen year old sit on a real one, yet have to wait another two years to enjoy or purchase a plastic toy one?

Do these plastic one's spread S.T.D's?

Do they prematurely ejaculate at the wrong time?

Do they get young girls pregnant?

Why not a toy before real sex then?

Everything is so fucked up !!

Take prisons for instance. They bang on about not having any more room inside these places and are constantly worrying about over-crowding. Okay, here's a really stupid idea – How about make a prison a fucking prison then?

Today prisons have sky TV, internet access, classrooms and sports halls. I mean, who is really scared to be locked up these days?

If I go on a boys night-out in Newcastle, after adding up the travel, hotel, drink and other stuff, you are dead broke. Fuck it, lets have a boys night-out in prison – Everything paid for, entertainment, things to do, no rent or tax to pay - It really is Butlins, but the FREE version.

Make a prison a prison. One steel bed, no friends, shitty food and hardly ever get out of your cell – Lets see who wants to go to prison then !!

Don't get me wrong, I know why the government do it this way. It's basically to keep everyone in the country happy and in this case, human-rights people. (Hey, nothing like keeping everyone happy to buy a vote, is there?) Well, what I say is...

Fuck Human-Rights...

If a criminal is big enough to kill or rape, then they're big enough to take full responsibility !!

It's simply the way of the world today and why things keep getting out of hand. I mean, what can teachers do these days? They can't even break-up a fight now, in-case they are taken to count for touching a child. (It's just as well Mrs Steward was an old lady back in my day, because she'd be at one of these holiday-camps, serving time if she was still teaching today)

It's getting that bad, that even the police have forgotten how to police. Wow, back in my day, you only had to say the word shit...

"*That's it son, you're nicked*"

Now I see kids on the street mocking them, swearing at them, boasting that they can't touch them because they are under-age, what is the world coming too?

Here's another idea Mr Government...

If you get kids like this, if they keep laughing at respectable Mr Policeman and degrading his authority, then lock their fucking parents up. (Hey, if they can't control their kids, why not?)

The world is changing...

Teachers can't teach, police can't police, but I think the worst change has got to be the doctor.

I don't do the doctor, not because I don't get sick, but because I know what they're going to say before they've even said it.

They are rubbish these days !!

If it's not bad enough you've got to pre-plan when you're going to be sick, so you can make an appointment three weeks in advance to see one of the fuckers, they then only give you five minutes of their superior medical advice. Something like this...

"*Don't worry Mr Perrin, you'll be fine in a few days*"

Thanks for that doctor knob-head, but I think I already worked that out myself, seeing as I've already been sick for two weeks without your help anyway and knew if it was serious, I would have taken myself to the fucking hospital.

I wouldn't mind, but you know that amazing, technical medical advice they give you? It isn't coming from their years of knowledge or medical experience any more, It's coming from the internet.

I've always wondered what they type in on their screen as they talk to you, I always thought they were filling in your records or something. Oh no, they're typing in exactly what you are telling them and letting the internet make it's own diagnoses.

I don't use a doctors name any more, I just call them all "*Doctor Google*"

Really? Is that what you wait two weeks for?

Something I could have done myself at home?

Saying that, I don't self diagnose either. Wow, have you tried it?

I've got a slight swelling around my eye, probably where I've been writing so much, or not been sleeping enough – Lets ask the internet.

Lets fucking not !!

How comes it doesn't matter what you type in or how minor, the bastard diagnoses always tries to kill you off? Fuck me, I only asked the internet the best way of removing strawberry milkshake from my favourite jumper and I've got to go straight to hospital for a life saving operation !!

Another thing I found bizarre visiting the doctors a few months ago (For the first time in something like eight years) They've now got these self-service, scan yourself in machines. It's a bit like self check-in at the airport, but you don't have to report to the receptionist when you arrive at the doctors.

Here's the sign that went with the machine

To save time, why not book yourself in using our self-service machine.

Fair enough, right?

If you have any problems or need assistance using it, please ask the receptionist.

Hold on a minute, this can't be right !!

I can walk in, over to the desk, whisper my name to the receptionist and be sitting in my seat within thirty seconds.

OR

I could fuck about with a machine, find out it doesn't work properly, walk over to the receptionist (Who the machine helps you avoid in the first place) then ask her to explain what all the buttons mean, which would take a lot longer me thinks, than whispering my fucking name to her in the first place !!

Save time? More like trying to make human-being's redundant, just like those stupid self-service tills at the supermarket.

One, there supposed to be there to make your shopping experience better and two, it's a way of cutting staffing hours and making the machine do all the work.

How the fuck is it working?

No sooner have you self scanned your first fucking item, all these lights start flashing, alarms go off and the machine crashes.

Then what happens?

Retarded Norman comes over, swipes his card, gives you a funny smile, then makes you look thicker than him because he can do it and you can't.

One thing...

Is he paid to rush over to everyone that crashes the self-service till? Then why not put him on a till and stop wasting our

fucking time !!

CHAPTER 9
ME, ME, ME

Oops, I'm meant to be talking about me, my writing and parts of my life, aren't I? Sorry, I get a little sidetracked when I get a bee in my bonnet about something.

"So what else can I tell you about me?"

Well, firstly I guess I should tell you I'm quite a private person, so you shouldn't expect too much information out of me. Hey, that's a good one, isn't it? A book about me, where I refuse to tell you anything about me (Can't be bad value for money, can it?) I can't help it. I guess it comes from a lifetime of being judged by people.

Fuck, do I hate being judged !!

I believe that everyone in life should be given the chance to prove themselves. I can't stand people that make up their mind about you or think they know you before they in-fact get to know you. Saying that, it's even worse when you have people that have known you a long time and still they insist they know you better than you know yourself.

"I know you Jimmy. There's no way you'd turn your nose up at a best seller or million pound book deal"

WOULDN'T I, REALLY?

When people judge me like this or think they know me, all it says to me is they don't know me at all.

So for those people that have said it since I started writing, let me repeat it one final time and make it clear for you.

*"I am in no-way a money driven person or materialistic for that matter. To me, the most important thing in life is love and happiness. I wouldn't swap these two things in my life for any amount of money... Yes a best seller would be nice, but as long as my book makes just **ONE** single person smile, I will continue to write and be happy"*

It's funny, but I know even writing this statement in the book, won't alter their opinion of me and they'll still think they know me better than I know myself.

"Yeah I know you wrote it in your book Jimmy, but I still don't believe you"

With some people, there's just no winning, but I guess that's why they don't get to see or experience the real me.

Me, I take pride in the people I care about and I am VERY fussy who I let into my life. Recently I have let two new people get to know me much better and although it's only been a short time, they've both accepted me for me and don't judge. In return these two people now know me better than those judgemental people that have been around me forever and they will get so much more from me because of it.

So, what have we got so far?

The jobs I've done in my life, a little about my writing, my dislike of small talk, my hatred for bullies or fake people and the fact I am very fussy with who I let into my life.

Okay, lets go backwards and talk about my writing again.

Who are my influences? Who inspires me?

Well firstly, my wife and children. You'll notice throughout this book I won't talk about them much, simply because I've been instructed to write this book in my style (comedy) and I can't write anything about them without getting all emotional or sentimental.

But they are my true inspiration and the reason I can do what I do. Basically, to write comedy you've got to be in a good place and be really happy all the time - I write comedy **EVERYDAY !!**

My parents for their love and support and for being proud of me.

My good friends (Yes, the one's that actually know me) for their love and support. One in particular I call "*Sticky*" who means the world to me and puts a **HUGE** smile on my face every day !!

Wow, this is sounding like some kind of awards ceremony now, isn't it? Okay, quicker, quicker, who or what are my influences?

The TV programme "*Two and a half men*" Massive fan.

Lee Evans,

Jim Davidson,

Martin Lawrence and Steve Carrell.

Who I admire?

Robson Green,

Marti Pellow,

Bruce Willis,

Shakira & Justin Timberlake.

Fast enough?

Pick one of them, the most influential?

UP YOUR BUM !!

Why? Who's going to make me?

My favourite colour is pink, my lucky number is twenty-six... Favourite food is pasta, favourite drink is milkshake... Unless of course I am drinking, drinking - Then it's Rum or Malibu (Yeah go on say it – Not exactly a drinking, drink for a man, is it?) I really only watch comedy or chick-flick films & don't do horrors.

My favourite actors are,

Bruce Willis,

Steve Carrell and Ashton Kutcher.

My favourite actresses are,

Amanda Peet,

Jennifer Aniston and Cameron Diaz.

"Er..."

Favourite film of all time?

"A lot like love"

Music?

Oh music, where do I start?

Michael Jackson is what I grew up with and still love today, but I enjoy any kind of music from 90's band Hanson, Busted to Mcfly and Justin Timberlake today. If I had to pick one all time favourite group, it would be Wet Wet Wet.

Favourite song ever?

Don't laugh you bastards – "Everytime" by Britney Spears

Okay, getting sidetracked again... My writing, writing, writing...

Do I plan out or plot my book?

"Yes, all my books are planned out from start to finish, before I actually start writing them. Well, except this one as you can tell, because I'm pretty much making it up as I go"

Do I get writer's block?

"NEVER... Sorry it doesn't happen to me – Although not knowing what I am going to write next right now, could be my first time"

Are any of my characters based on me or real people?

"Again, no not really. I just visualise the character and their personality, then watch what happens as it unfolds in my head"

"I do however place a celebrity face to every character I write, which helps me visualise, but again it doesn't resemble those people in real life or a character they may or may not have played before"

You want to know who my characters are now, don't you?

Okay...

Malcolm – I visualise Steve Carrell.

Dexter – Has always been Martin Lawrence.

Sally – Is Surranne Jones.

Becky – I think was Halle Berry.

Okay, maybe not them all, as I didn't have one for Mrs Pufflewoo, but come on, who can't visualise an eighty year old mad Chinese woman?

Yasmin Pufflewoo – Was Kristin Kreuk.

Mike Hunt (The fireman) Is Bradley cooper.

And the new character coming up in the third book called Candy, will be visualised in my head as Ariana Grande.

I won't go through people in my other books, but as you can see, I always put a face to my characters, just so I can write it easier.

How long will the Hard Up series run for?

"The series will run for as long as people want to read it. Readers of the first two are already waiting for the third, I myself am currently plotting the fourth, so who knows? I guess as long as I keep finding things for Malcolm and Dexter to get into mischief with, I can write them"

My writing ambition?

"I'm not really sure as my ultimate ambition was to start writing a book and finish it. I guess I wouldn't mind doing a film over in America one day, but REALLY, anything that happens with my writing now will always be just a bonus"

Like I said before, as long as you've got happiness and love in your life, nothing else really matters !!

CHAPTER 10
WRITER'S BLOCK & SCOTLAND

OH DEAR – FOR THE FIRST TIME EVER, I'M EXPERIENCING
WRITERS BLOCK.

*"Hey, how lucky do you feel? My first time experience
and I am sharing it with you"*

I have absolutely no idea what question about my writing I should
answer next, so I will just elaborate on what I have said before...

I don't see myself as an author, I'm simply just someone that
writes shit down, then gets all kinds of overwhelmed when people
like what I am writing. I'm not joking, it really does overwhelm me.
Why would anyone like anything I have to say?

"Er..."

"Er..."

Still suffering writers block...

"Er..."

"Er..."

Fuck, I wish I could ask someone what they want me to answer
next, because I am blank !!

Saying that, I would ask **ANYONE** but my friend *"Sticky"*

See, *"Sticky"* hates someone asking for a question, when that question isn't there, then the question for a question becomes a pressure to ask a bloody question.

Confused? You know what I mean, don't you *"Sticky?"*

You better know what I am talking about, otherwise this part of my writing becomes pointless and I might as well explain how you got yourself the nickname *"Sticky"* instead.

(Ooh, Shall I?)

See, what I did there readers? If my writing can make just one person smile or laugh, that's all I need to continue writing and I know right now *"Sticky"* won't be able to wipe the smile away.

(Smile or nervous embarrassment, not sure which one just yet)

I guess that depends on whether or not I go through the whole *"Sticky"* story for you.

Okay, lets go to the section where I made my transition from growing up in London, then moving to Scotland in much more detail. (Fuck knows why I said much more detail, I haven't even told you this part yet, have I?)

See, that's another reason why a writer must plan out a book, because the daft idiot writer won't know what he's already told you.

I moved from the City of London and from a town called Battersea to Scotland when I was just nineteen, I think... Eighteen or nineteen, who's keeping track?

When I say moved, I actually drove up with my family in the removal truck, got as far as Dundee (Which was another two hundred or so miles away from our new home) and turned back.

Ever heard anything like this before?

Homesick before someone actually reaches their new destination?

Okay, maybe not homesick, but the further north we drove, the more things changed and I didn't like it.

First the busy traffic jams of London turned into miles and miles of green fields. (Why did I feel the need to say green? Of course they're bloody green) Anyway, first came the fields, then came the cows, before all hell broke loose...

What happened next?

Well all the street names and signs started to disappear.

This is **REALLY** what put me off Scotland on my very first visit !!

(Miles and miles of road and not one sign to tell you where you are) How would you ever find your way around? How the fuck would you give someone directions?

"Yeah, drive north, pass about the hundredth tree, then it's first on your left pass the random highland cow"

SO, after the ten odd hour drive up to Scotland, I drove all the way down again, hopefully to work out where I was going to live now. Saying that, I was so bored of sitting in that fucking truck, I would have stopped anywhere and set up home.

I ended up living down in Folkestone, then six months later decided to go and visit my family back up in Scotland for the weekend. On this particular weekend, I still didn't like the place, but something happened, or should I say changed? After walking miles and miles through fields just to reach the local village and a single shop, I met my wife. I say I met her over the weekend, but it was more like during the first few hours of being there and I've been with her and living up here ever since.

(Go on, say it – *Ahhhhh*, love at first sight)

"Ahhhhh, ahhhhh, fucking HA – Shove your ahhhhh up your bloody arse !!"

"Love at first sight? More like, wow, I hope all the girls up here are this easy"

Hey, it's not like London where there's something like one woman to every six million men, this was like one girl, one boy, a shit load of cows and a barn in the middle of nowhere – What wasn't to stick around for?

Okay, at first I still had a lot of acclimatising to do, but as long as I could find my way over to that village in the dark, without being attacked by some wild fucking animal, I think I could adapt.

Me and the wife have been together now for twenty-one years and married for...

"Er? Yeah, a very long time"

(Only joking, sixteen years)

SIXTEEN "LLLOOOOOONNNNNGGGG" YEARS...

(Unless of course you are reading this book years after it's release, in which case it's a lot bloody longer)

SO MUCH LLLOOOOOONNNNNGGGGER !!

We got married in Gretna Green, which is the place that people run off to get married in and although we did kind of run off to get married, we didn't exactly run off.

Confused? Thought you might be, well let me explain...

"Wow, wouldn't it be funny if I didn't?"

Although we didn't invite anyone to the wedding - Because of my job, we actually lived down near Gretna at that time anyway. See, we didn't run anywhere, we just forgot to invite people !!

Our wedding day was probably the worst day of my life. Oops that sounds bad, doesn't it?

Our wedding day **WAS** the worst day of my life. That's better !!

Not worst as in bad, but worst as in shove a butt-plug up my anus and call me nervous !!

I have no idea how anyone can get married in front of a crowd of people and that's me, ex-redcoat and public reading writer saying this.

(Reading writer? Wow, now there's two words I didn't think you'd be able to fit together into a sentence – Hey, maybe they don't fit and that just proves how crap I am at my job)

I shook, I trembled, almost passed out. I hated it.

My nerves were that bad on my wedding day, that I don't actually remember the wife being there herself !!

Anyway, one REALLY good thing came out of the day and that was (No, not getting married) I got to pick the date. What an anniversary to have...

(The 26th May)

As in **M** for **M**ay, or the other **M** month being in **M**arch, which happens to be my birthday too...

(The 26th March)

See? First 26th **M** in the month, my birthday - Second 26th **M**, wedding anniversary.

I so love being the one not to forget our special day and it proves I'm not just a pretty face.

(No, I'm a devious little bastard too)

I said I wouldn't talk about my wife or kids throughout this book, because it would upset me and although I won't mention my **WONDERFUL** (Reason I live) children, I must say something else about my wife. She understands me better than anyone I know, she truly knows me inside out and I don't think I would cope a single day without her. We've got an amazing relationship and we are always on the same wavelength.

Same wavelength being...

"I support her fully, she leans on me"

"I make all the hard decisions in life, she takes all the credit"

"I do all the funny, she takes all the laughs"

You know, I would actually feel a little worried about getting into trouble at this stage, but I can't be bothered to tell myself off on her behalf.

No Really, She's My Rock !!

(Yeah, the rock that rots your teeth)

She's My Everything !!

(Sorry, I mean, I'm her everything)

She's Amazing !!

(At cooking)

Fuck this is like one of those fights you have trying to get the last word, yet doing it with yourself !!

(BACK TO SCOTLAND)

Although this country is probably one of the most beautiful places on the planet, it took me a good few years to finally call it home. First I did manage to find another road sign or street name – Hey, they were there all the time.

No, not hidden behind a huge oak tree in the middle of the forest, but right there in the A to Z map book.

Saying that, as soon as I found out what the places were called, I wish I never, because I couldn't bloody say them, let alone read them.

"Drumlithie"

"Migvie"

"Colnabaichin"

"Auchininna"

And my favourite...

"Fochabers"

"Mr spell-check & Mr grammar, I know you love telling me when I've messed up, but you're going to have to trust me on this one, because they are all real places and words"

How was a teenager meant to swap the likes of Clapham, Wandsworth and Lambeth for names like Fochabers?

"Fuck-a-what?"

"That's it son, you're nicked"

"Oh bollocks, what again? I was only asking for directions"

Another thing I had to get used to up in Scotland was the winters, or more to the point, the snow. Hey, this is someone who grew-up in London, who'd only ever seen snow once in his life.

Blizzards, snow drifts, four foot of the stuff to wade through – I remember the first time I experienced it, I thought I was going to die !!

The final thing it took me ages to adjust to was the Scottish accent. Wow, talk about speaking a different language in English (If that makes sense) Up here it's all,

"Fitya dee'in min? Aye, ya gaun doon the toon in this caul or gauna bide at hem?"

Hey, look at that, I wrote something in Scottish – Maybe I can speak it better than I actually thought I could, or is it just easier to write? Either way, I struggled like crazy with this living up here.

So, how did I overcome all these little things?

Simple answer is – **I didn't !!**

After nearly twenty years of living in Scotland, I still haven't got used to it and instead taught myself ways round it.

I never try to say the big confusing places any more, simply because I can't, so instead I go to the nearest town I can pronounce and say that instead... Fochabers? Fuck off, now it's that place starting with F up near Elgin – See?

The snow, well there's no getting away from the snow in the winter, so I simply wear more clothes or don't go out in it.

And the accent? Well here's the thing...

I've now taught myself that if I don't understand something, I can either go with "*Fit*" which means what, "*Aye*, which means yes, or "*O'aye*" which means you agree and sound a little bit like a farmer from Nolfolk.

Usually if I don't understand anything at all, it's an "*O'aye*" from me, because at least I am agreeing with what the person is talking about so passionately.

(I CAN ONLY IMAGINE THE STICK I'M GOING TO GET FOR EXPLAINING THIS)

Can I talk Scottish?

Sort of...

You've heard of Scottish whiskey, right? The Scotch egg?

Well me, I'm the...

Scotch cock !!

It's what I call myself when I try to speak Scottish, then it comes out half London cockney too.

"*Aye, Aye, Al-right then mate, Aye, yeah, I will be doon to play fit-ball soon, but I dinna kin fit time... Aye, yeah, see you later mush, nice one Harry*"

Hey, told you, I'm one of a kind !!

Although I love this country and am VERY proud to be a part of it, I think the only thing that gets me down from time to time is the prejudice. It really is a pile of crap...

Don't get me wrong, it's not about the Scottish people against the English, or the English against the Scottish, it's just what it's built up to sound like. Most of my best friends are Scottish and they don't have a problem with where I come from, but there are just a few that hold onto the memory of William Wallace and take it a little too far.

As you know, it takes a lot to push those buttons of mine, but come on... When you have a mouthy seventeen year old giving you lip because of where you come from, it does from time to time get you down.

"Get over it you immature Twat, I've been living up here longer than you've been alive"

I get it already, I understand Mr Wallace fought the English for an independent Scotland – Fuck, if I was Scottish and alive back then, I would have joined in and beaten up the Guff bastards too, but we're not – This is 2014, so grow the fuck up, Jock !!

"Oops !!"

Saying that, if I only lived in London for eighteen years of my life and have been up here longer now, doesn't that sort of pass me fit for acceptance anyway?

Scotland is a wonderful place, with a wonderful culture. My wife is from here, my children were born here and I wouldn't want to live anywhere else in the world !!

I think if there's just one single thing I could change, it would be the mobile phone coverage and internet service – It's rubbish !!

I mean, you'd actually think it would be better, wouldn't you? Miles and miles of countryside, with plenty of space to put those satellite transmitter things.

CHAPTER 11
TECHNOLOGY

Lucky for me I ain't one for mobile phones, or answering them when they ring for that matter, as it's been pointed out **SO** many times before. Nope, give me something that has buttons on it, that rings and I'm just fine. I mean, why do we need all these features on phones these days? Who needs a fucking App for the weather? Er, I know, go outside your house and see what it's like for yourself you lazy sod !!

Just like people and professions are changing in this day and age, so too is technology and I for one, can't stand it. Don't get me wrong, I'm glad the old fashioned tape playing Walkman was replaced by a CD player, then I'm glad that has now been replaced by an MP3 too, but when does it stop? There's nothing better to me than having my headphones in all day long and getting down to the Wets, but even the MP3 is changing and upgrading itself now. The last one I bought myself not only had a MP3 feature on it (Which is the reason I purchased it in the first place) but it had a built in camera, social networking buttons and loads of other crap on it. If I wanted to buy a fucking camera, I would have bought a fucking camera !!

Have you got any idea how long it takes it wipe off all these unwanted features?

Unwanted features that take up memory by the way, that prevents you from putting as much fucking music on your music player as you wanted to do in the first place? ARSE-BAGS !!

And what about the car satellite navigation system or (Sat-Nav) as it's called?

You know, me and the wife used to love travelling up and down the UK, having our own little adventure.

Where's the adventure now?

"At the next junction in exactly two hundred feet, turn left"

Fuck off !!

Don't you understand that half the fun of going on those adventures was about getting lost? What's the point of going for a long drive now, if you know you're going to get to your destination in one piece? I mean, getting lost, turning off at the wrong junction, driving in the wrong direction for sixty miles, caused so many arguments in the past. So many good arguments in-fact, that we had to stop overnight in a hotel to have aggressive argumentative sex all the time. What's the point now?

"You've reached your destination"

Whoopee, great job Sat-Nav... Now lets check into the hotel, crash out because your calming fucking voice has made us relax so much and forget the passion, you... cock sucking pile of shit machine.

Guess what – We don't have a car any more !!

So I guess by this stage you think I'm a grumpy old fucker, that moans about everything I don't like in the world. No, that's not true. I'm a VERY happy and positive person, that likes to grump about things I don't like in the world.

Who am I? I guess if you know me like my real friends do, you'd think I was a nice guy. I'm always happy, always laughing, always messing about. I'm loyal, trustworthy and sensitive.

"*A Big Softy*" is what most people call me, although I don't like this statement either, because the "*BIG*" part of the "*Big Softy*" makes me want to diet all the time and lose weight.

"Hey, what do you expect, I just told you I was fucking sensitive"

I guess what makes me different is I don't act like most guys. Whilst they walk around trying to look all hard, then save the world in a macho way, I just sit back and chill... Don't get me wrong, I wear my Bruce Willis vest under my top just in-case I get the call, but I don't feel I've got anything to prove to anyone.

I know who I am, I know what I am capable of doing and I only do it when required of me.

I guess I at this point, it would have been easier to say I wear my heart on my sleeve, but where's the fun in that? Hey, I'm trying to write a longish book about myself here, not get to the end as fast as I can !!

CHAPTER 12
SENSITIVE

I'll tell you how sensitive I can be.

My cousin came to visit me a few months back from London.

I decided to take him to the theatre in Edinburgh to watch a show. Now you all know I like chick-flick films and stuff like that, but I bought tickets to watch Evita. Straight away I thought this is even too girlie for me, but seeing as one of my heroes Marti Pellow was performing in it, I thought what the hell.

I REALLY didn't expect to enjoy a soppy love story, some weird aggressive political thing, but I did. The music was dramatic, Marti's voice was incredible as usual and I loved every second.

There's me a bald headed hard-nut sitting there, my gay cousin, surrounded by hundreds of O.A.P's for the afternoon show and who was the one that had to hold back the most emotion?

Fuck I hate it when this happens !!

You feel the lump in your throat getting bigger and bigger.

You don't want to sniff or swallow in-case someone hears or looks at you.

Then the more you hold back, the more the sweat starts to drip from your forehead.

(Which incidentally, makes you look like you're crying, even though your fucking not)

It was terrible. I think I must have clapped twenty percent of the time, held back seventy percent, which means I only actually watched ten percent of the entire show. I wouldn't mind, but I thought I got away with it when it ended, then my cousin was quick enough to tell me he actually noticed me holding back and fighting it. I wish he would have told me during it, because then I wouldn't have had to put myself through the whole choking up ordeal.

Yes I'm a big softy, but that's only my disguise for when people press my buttons. Where other guys act all tough and shit, then hide their sensitivity inside – I let my sensitive side shine out and hide the crazy-arse, don't fuck with me lunatic I am underneath.

I guess it's all a part of being a good parent, wanting to be the perfect role model for my children and talking of role models, here's something else that does my head in.

THE BLOODY ROLE MODEL

I am absolutely sick fucking tired of hearing these people on the TV slagging off celebrities because they are bad role models.

Britney Spears has had it for years, Rihanna too and recently Miley Cyrus.

What's wrong with these nagging (Haven't got anything better to do) people? Why can't you leave these celebrities alone?

Okay, lets take a closer look at these celebrities

Britney got caught in a photograph wearing no knickers, then kissed another female on stage. Rihanna likes to dress in as little as possible and gyrates all over the place. And Miley shakes her behind in a new thing called the twerk and gets off licking her lips.

Great, what's your problem?

Is it really Britney's problem that she's sexual and liberated enough not to wear underwear? Is it her fault some perverted photographer points his camera right between her legs? Okay then, have you never done anything risky in your life for the benefit of a partner or your sex life? Ah see, that's the point, most of us have done exactly the same thing, but the only difference is, we're not exposed in the same way a celebrity is.

I mean, what does it come down to? Are your children really looking at these three celebrities and idealising them as role models? Does your daughter really want to dress in fewer clothes or go out without pants on?

Get a grip !!

The only reason you've got the hump is because you're getting older and you can't pull this kind of stuff off yourself any more. Here's an idea – If you don't like your kids watching people like this, turn your TV the fuck off then !!

What these celebrities are becoming is scapegoats. Scapegoats for you not wanting to take responsibility for your own kids actions. Therefore any time one of your children do something wrong, it's easier for you to blame the likes of Britney.

"*Hey, my daughter was out last week and got caught shoplifting. It's all that celebrities fault*"

Really? That's the best you can do?

Oh okay then, it's the celebrities fault because they may or may not have done it back in 1980... Not uncle Tim's fault (You know your brother) the one that committed armed robbery on a bank only a few months ago.

See if there's one thing I know, it's EVERY single family in the world has their problems and EVERY family will have a bad role model in there somewhere. So, why aren't you blaming that person? Haven't you got a sister, cousin or someone related to you that dresses nice and slutty?

What about a friend you hang about with?

Really, are they all ugly prudes like you?

Shouldn't these people be more a role model for your kids than your chosen scapegoat celebrity?

Bottom line is, leave them alone and get a life. That celebrity you keep targeting is a human-being just like you. Instead of blaming the world and the role models influencing your children, take responsibility yourself.

I say this with confidence for one reason – I love my children more than life itself and although I know they all enjoy their own kind of celebrities and fashions, I AM THE ONLY ROLE MODEL THEY NEED. Not cousin Tina who dresses like a slag-bag, not uncle Bert who is a criminal, not those celebrities they watch on TV – JUST ME !!

END OF RANT !!

"Wow, that was a good one, wasn't it?"

Sorry if I offended anyone. I didn't mean to call you ugly before. I was just remarking on your ugly personality and attitudes towards celebrities, not your looks. Don't suppose that makes you scapegoat users feel any better, does it?

Oh well, lets move on quickly then...

CHAPTER 13
SHOPPING

Oh crap, just when I say quickly, I get another writers block...

"Er..."

"Er..."

"Er..."

Stop thinking about calling people ugly.

"Er..."

"Er..."

They won't be offended if you move on quickly.

"Er..."

I know, lets do one for the girls - Lets do a section on shopping, yeah that won't offend anyone much, will it?

"Er..."

Shopping? Okay, here it comes, shopping...

How comes it's always said that men can't shop or they don't like to shop?

Every man I know enjoys shopping, including me. The only thing we can't stand is doing it with a female. See, it's not that we don't like to shop, it's that we aren't allowed to shop.

Don't like, not allowed...

Two completely different things !!

Here's how just one of those shopping trips would go for me

"Hey Jimmy, do you fancy coming shopping? Come on, you can buy yourself anything you like today"

"Anything? Oh, al-right then"

(PROBLEM 1 – ENTERING THE SHOP)

"Okay, see you in a minute, I will catch you up"

Why is it a problem that we men have already mapped out where we're going to head first, before we've actually entered the shop? I mean, Is it a crime?

"Oh, okay then, if you want to bugger off and leave me"

Or

"Fine, if you're too embarrassed to be seen with me in public"

Or better still...

"Heading towards the cakes and doughnuts, are you fatty?"

Obviously not bloody now I'm not !!

"No, it's okay, I'll walk beside you and push the fucking trolley... Mum"

(PROBLEM 2 – PICKING OUT SOMETHING TO BUY)

"I will have a box of these cakes, no in-fact, make that two"

Wrong, so wrong !!

"You do know we're on a food shop, don't you? As in food, food shop and not your cakes, biscuit and chocolate food shop?"

Food, food? What the fuck is food, food?

I'll tell you what food, food is...

Food, food is all that crap a man will pick up and shove in the trolley that the wife or girlfriend doesn't see worthy of purchase or consumption. And furthermore, it's all that food we're going to pig out on, that she can't eat, because of the latest fucking diet she's putting herself through.

"Oh, okay then darling. I will just pick up some food, food, like this lovely tin of peas"

Which may I add, won't be something I ever go to the kitchen cupboard for, or choose to snack on late at night.

"No, I didn't mean it that way. You can have whatever you like"

Have what I like? You've just made me put two boxes of my favourite cakes back !!

"Just buy something you really want. I mean, do you actually like those two boxes of fairy cakes you've just shoved into the trolley without thinking?"

Yes in-fact, I bloody do !!

(PROBLEM 3 – PICKING ANYTHING ELSE UP)

"Okay then, I'll just go with the one box of cakes"

"Well, if you're sure. You can have more if you want"

"No it's okay, this one box will do"

"Shame"

Shame?

Where did the shame come from? I shoved in two boxes, got nagged, now I've only got one and it's a shame, why?

"No it's just, if you bought these one's last week, they were on special offer"

Last week? I'm fucking shopping now, not last week !!

"You know I like looking out for the special offers and saving a little bit of money"

Well, if it makes you feel better, I'll will happily pay the ten pence difference.

(Oh no) - (No, no, no, no, no – There's no way we could possibly say that)

Nope, instead we agree on the huge effect that ten pence is going to make to our lives, put our favourite cakes back on the shelf and search out the fooshty one on special offer to please her.

(PROBLEM 4 – THE SMILE)

Once we have the single box of special offer cakes, that we didn't want in the first place and this shopping trip has been completely shit so far - We struggle to look interested any more, as she happily checks the dates on the yoghurt and shovels two million of the things into the trolley.

Then comes the kick in the balls,

THE REALLY **BIG** KICK IN THE BALLS !!

"You know, if you didn't want to come out shopping, you only had to say"

That's funny love, because I thought the words *"Neah"* when you offered, sounded quite straight forward and direct to me !!

You force a smile, but that one's not good enough, so do it again, but the fucking cartoons of yoghurt have squashed your fooshty special offer cake, so you feel the need to say something...

"Why do we need all this yoghurt?"

"It will get eaten, don't you worry about that"

"Yeah, but don't you think there's like, a smidgen too much?"

"Who does the shopping every week?"

"Who knows exactly what we need?"

"If I say it will get eaten, then it will get eaten"

At this moment in time, you're biting your tongue so fucking hard, that the (**Special Offer**) of oral sex tonight is threatening to leap off the table and you're dying to tell the bitch you've just started a **SPECIAL** yoghurt free fucking diet...

So with no food in the trolley, plenty of food, food and just one squashed cake to lighten our shopping trip, down the cosmetic isle we go...

"Ooh deodorant and look, my favourite one is on special offer too"

Surely now, we've got something right?

Have we bollocks !!

(PROBLEM 5 – NOTHING WE WANT IS GOOD ENOUGH)

In go the two tins of deodorant, out come the two tins of deodorant.

"That's my favourite, I've run out at home and there on special offer, so why are you taking them back out of the trolley?"

"Yeah but..."

*"**Yeah but, I can get them down the high-street for a pound less anyway**"*

Then what the fuck are we walking down this isle for?

*"**How about I finish up the food shopping and you go and get yourself a new shirt?**"*

Really? You're going to trust me to get something myself? Saying that, when did the food, food shopping turn back into the food shopping again?

(PROBLEM 6 – YOUR CHOICE ISN'T YOUR CHOICE)

Men's section, clothes, no women, surely this is all about me enjoying myself now? Yeah - Right up until you've fallen in love with a certain shirt and she comes over.

*"**Really? You like that one? Haven't you got one like that already?**"*

Well duh... That's why I really like it.

*"**MM'mm, yeah, no, I'm not sure**"*

You're not sure? It's my new fucking shirt !!

*"**Why don't you go and try it on in the changing room and see if it fits you first**"*

"It'll fit"

*"**Yeah well if it doesn't, you'll be the one bringing it back and exchanging it**"*

"Yeah, of course I will"

Not !!

She holds it up to you, pulls a few funny faces, then makes a few more thinking noises.

*"**You know what, I think I've seen something like this before**"*

"Yeah I know, I've got one like it – I thought we already discovered this bit?"

"No, I mean on Ebay"

OH FUCK,

IT'S NOT HAMMER TIME, IT'S EBAY TIME !!

"Why don't you leave it for now, see what I can find on the internet and if I can't find anything, you can come back and buy it"

Come back and buy it? I don't plan to come back here, EVER !!

By this time, you either want to kill the bitch, go and wait in the car or better still, fuck her to death... Ooh, there's an idea.

"You see that changing room over there?"

"Well I thought me and you, you know, could..."

"Don't be so disgusting, this is a supermarket, not our bedroom"

Yeah, like I get much action in there either, playing gooseberry to your laptop and all those fucking shopping sites !!

It doesn't matter what we do or what we pick up, it's always going to be wrong.

A DVD perhaps? You know, to cuddle up in bed and watch together tonight?

"Haven't we already seen that one?"

A new blender for her instead, just to get in her good books again?

"What you trying to say, I belong in the kitchen?"

Nothing we do out shopping with our other half is good enough and the bottom line is, any time we do get ourselves out there, we never get what we were promised. (You can buy anything you like indeed) – Yeah right, so how comes I've got a single fooshty cake, probably a cake that you will eat half of anyway and a fucking headache?

Men like shopping girls, but let them fucking shop !!

CHAPTER 14
FOOTBALL

Okay, I've moaned enough now, so I think it's time I told you a little more about myself. blimey, what's next? How about sport?

(Ha, not one for the girls this time)

I've always been quite a sporty person, although as you know, not very good at it until I started teaching it and got good playing against kids. I think my favourite sports have got to be between swimming, badminton, football and rugby, but I don't know in which order.

I've been a die-hard West Ham fan since I can remember and used to go to the matches at Upton Park with my best friend when I was younger and lived in London. When I say a die-hard fan, I don't mean like these fans that live and breath football and know every song they sing in the stands word for word. Although I obviously know "I'm forever blowing bubbles" which I've been trying to teach my children for years and is probably the reason why they all support Newcastle now.

West Ham to me is like a part of my history, a part of me that can't be changed and although I live up in Scotland now, I am very proud to be a hammer. Saying that, they've never been a top team in the league and lose more games than they can win. That's always been a thing of mine (See, loyalty again) I don't care what happens to the team, how many games they lose or whether they turn into a netball set-up, I would still follow and support them.

Playing football myself started at the age of ten with a team in Clapham called *"The Ambers"* I then played for my dad's teams *"Dunstone"* and *"Clapham Wanderers"* before ditching his team and joining *"Trinity"* in Wandsworth. I think it was only here in this team that I started to improve and build my confidence. It wasn't that my dad wasn't a good manager (Because he was one of the best) but I think stepping away helped me mature and grow-up a little - Either that, or stop fucking around with the friends I grew-up with in my dad's team.

Throughout my teens I played for professional clubs such as *"Folkestone"* and *"Carshalton"* but my favourite playing days didn't come until I moved to Scotland and joined *"Monymusk"*

(Remember that little village my wife lived in? The one that I had to walk miles to find? The one that only had a little shop? Well they also had a football team – Yes with all eight villagers)

I played with this team on and off for a good three or four years in the Scottish Amateur league. I did okay in the team and scored quite a few goals, but I think it was making so many good friends that made me want to stay season after season. My role in the team was striker (To score the goals) and although I tried my best to do my job, sometimes it just wasn't possible... Oh no, not because I couldn't score them, but because I ended up getting sent off all the time. Wow, did I have some cool punch-ups playing for that team? Proved one thing – Scottish football is tougher !!

(Either that, or they liked kicking

the shit out of an English dude)

After Monymusk I joined semi-professional side *"Huntly"* but didn't really enjoy my time there. Partly because I missed my old mates at the Musk and partly because these were real footballers and I was getting on a bit.

I rejoined *"Monymusk"* to have my final retirement football season at the age of...

(Yeah like I'm going to remember how old I was)

Anyway, this is the season I became somewhat of a celebrity in the village.

It was half way through the season and little village side Musk had been drawn in the Scottish cup final to play professional team Wick. This was probably the biggest game in the clubs history and all eight villagers were keeping their fingers crossed, we'd do well.

(When I say eight villagers, I actually mean around fifteen)

It was my job to score the goals, my job to help the team win this very important game and my job not to get dropped from the line-up and put on the subs bench !!

Hey, the bus trip up to Wick took fucking ages? (It's like right at the top of the UK) How was I supposed to know the team bus would have drink on board?

I got smashed !!

I don't know what was worse that day – Sitting on a bus for hours for nothing? Sitting on the sidelines watching the team play? Or the sobering headache I had by half time?

Twenty minutes of the game left and the score was level at nil, nil. Little Musk were holding their own against the mighty Wick. (Not that I watched much, as my head kept spinning around on the touchline)

Ten minutes to go, still nil, nil. Oh wait, time for a substitution.

"Who me? You want me to play? Really?"

Exactly twenty seconds after running onto the pitch a cross came in and I headed the winning goal (Which may I add, was probably one of the only times I actually used my head to score a goal) To be brutally honest, it was a long time ago now, but I still don't understand how little me jumped the highest and knocked it in, but the story of that day and night in Wick is still told by the villagers of Monymusk today.

Oh yeah, I forgot to tell you what happened that night, didn't I?

Well basically, we won the cup and because I had scored that famous goal, it was my job to drink from the trophy after lifting it. I tipped my head back and threw down a litre of champagne, knowing I could handle it.

(Turned out not to be champagne, but fucking whiskey)

"Hey, this don't taste like champagne"

They are the last words I remember saying before passing out within seconds. Don't worry though, two hours later I came round and partied hard into the night to celebrate that famous event.

"Who the fuck fills a trophy with whiskey?"

ANYWAY, that was the last competitive football match I played !!

As for swimming, well you know I used to teach it, but I love swimming myself too, especially diving. Rugby is not something I've played competitively, but I love the sheer aggression of it and badminton, well badminton became my replacement for football.

Which one do I spend most time doing?

"None really, I write all the time"

Which one is my favourite?

"I would have to say badminton, because I am really good at it"

Which one do I watch the most on TV?

"None... Hey I said I was into sport, not into watching it"

In-fact the only time you'll catch me watching sport on TV is when West Ham are playing or the Grand National is on. (They're the only two things I've never missed), which I guess doesn't make me as sporty as a real man after all, does it?

CHAPTER 15
AGE

Talking of Wick and that night out, here's something else about me that you might find interesting. I love to nightclub and I love to dance. (Okay, maybe not that interesting, but it's another fact about me at least)

Without sounding to cocky or up myself, I am good !!

Ever since I can remember (Well at least since I turned eighteen) all I've ever got is people praising me for my moves on the dance floor. I've even been at a point in time where I've walked into a club and the DJ has already got a song ready for me.

Granted I don't get out as much any more, but when I do, I do...

So why don't I get out as much any more? Simply - My friends !!

"Oh Jimmy, I couldn't possibly go out again. We were only out like ten months ago"

No, they aren't all boring, but they are starting to feel their age. Whereas me, well I'm eighteen forever... Okay maybe twenty-two (Ish) but I can still do it !!

It's a horrible fact, but as you get older, the fun times that you used to know start to fade away. As the people in nightclubs seemingly get younger and younger, It's in-fact you getting older and older that is the problem.

"How can we go out for a dance? The youngsters will laugh at us"

This is the kind of comment I get these days, yet I don't feel this way myself.

"What's it going to look like, us up there doing our dad dance?"

Dad dance? Speak for yourself shit-head, I can still bust-a-move !!

Well that's what I thought until the last time I went out

There's me out out on the dance floor, still trying to prove to the world I've got it and there's my friends all hanging about, scared to enjoy themselves. I rocked that night, I really did, yet it wasn't until after I got knackered and decided to take a break, that I knew things would never be the same again.

There's me getting all kinds of attention like I've been getting since my redcoat days and there's this hot young nineteen year old girl paying me compliments.

It wasn't until one of my friends got the hump and stepped in, did I realise things were about to change forever...

...

"So are you telling me, a young girl like you thinks Jimmy here is a good dancer"

"I sure do"

Good start, right?

"Yeah but is he a good dancer as in good dancer, or is he a good dancer like your dad?"

"That was the sexiest, hottest moves I've seen a man do in ages"

Could this night get any better? I mean, this was a hot nineteen year old paying bald, sweaty me a compliment.

"Just a shame, he's old"

BANG, THUD, CrASh !!

That was the sound of my ego, confidence, charm and jaw all hitting the floor at the same time. Can you believe it, whilst I was out there giving all my best moves and proving to my friends that you don't have to stop enjoying yourself, I'm told I am old.

Still, I won't let this deter me – I won't let it stop me.

(No, I will just go to clubs designed for older people next time)

With age comes a lot of stigma and with age comes that very famous saying...

"*Age is nothing but a number*"

What a pile of crap !!

Age IS a meaningful number, it's your fucking age !!

My advice to anyone trying to stay young or beat age, is to forget it. There's no winning, there's no fighting it – All you can really do is accept it.

"I now accept my age (Around twenty-five) and I concentrate on something else now"

See to me, the only thing that will keep you alive longer and feeling young is your brain. If you keep that healthy, don't bog your life down with boring routine, then if you do something complete nuts from time to time, this is how you will beat the ageing process.

No amount of wrinkle cream, make-up or cosmetic surgery is going to stop you getting older, yet if you keep that mind of yours ticking, you'll never feel as old as you are.

Great, my wife just read over that last part regarding what the nineteen year old said about me and ended with an "***Ahhhhh***"

"*What have I told you over the years about your ahhhhh's?*"

"*Ahhhhh's, calling me sweet and fucking cute don't suit my hard man personality, so stop it !!*"

"*I'll give you ahhhhh and stop you feeling sorry for me. Here's how I really feel about myself, thank you very much*"

I know I haven't got the biggest penis in the world, but it is MUCH bigger than the smallest one in the world.

...

I'm a lazy bastard sometimes... Yeah I will lay there for a good three hours, let you sit on top of me and go the duration.

...

You won't EVER hear me say I'm the best writer in the world – No, I will leave that to you.

...

I'm not the best lover in the world, but I'm certainly second best to myself next year.

Fuck those statements were really good, weren't they?

In-fact it was so good, I might have to get the copyright done.

In-fact one was that good, I want to say it again.

(Bet you can't guess which one I am going to pick)

I'm not the best lover in the world, but I'm certainly second best to myself next year.

Wow, how honest can one man be?

Before I move on from the age story and rant I just had, can I just say, sleep helps too. Something I clearly don't do enough of myself.

Fuck if I could sleep for eight to ten hours a night, my ageing process would slow down completely and I would easily pass for a seventeen year old.

See, I'm one of these people that only need four hours sleep and when I say need four hours sleep, that's all I can sleep for.

Bed at one in the morning, up at five (That's my usual routine)

Bed at three, up at seven.

You get the point, don't you?

Fuck it gets really silly when I'm tired early and fall asleep at seven. There's my eldest going to bed about eleven and I'm just getting up for the day.

Sometimes sleeping like this is a pain in the arse, sometimes it's a blessing. One, it means I can get up at silly o'clock and write without the chaotic household and two, it means I don't have to put up with the snoring wife all night long. Oops !!

On the downside, once I am up and my brain starts ticking, there's no shutting the sod off and I must keep going like a nut-job until everything is out or written down, which sometimes is exhausting.

I think the best part of sleeping in four hour shifts, is when people ask you that famous question...

*"**Are you a morning person or a night owl?**"*

"Er..."

The look on everyone's face when I tell them I am both.

"No, no, you can't, er... I asked, are you a morning or night person?"

"Yeah, I'm both. Super charged in the morning, party animal at night"

It's like they look at me as though I'm from a different planet sometimes. Saying that, you've got to know me, my humour and my personality better now, so you be the judge...

Planet Earth, Planet Flake or Planet up your anus?

(Be careful what you wish for !!)

CHAPTER 16
BUGGER

Okay, what else can I tell you? Ooh I know, that I used to be a jockey. Fuck, done that haven't I? Please don't make me read back through my writing, please – You know I hate fucking reading. What haven't I covered? What place haven't I been yet?

Ooh, there's a good one, places I haven't been, or better still, places where I've lived. (Although it would probably be quicker to tell you where I haven't stayed)

Okay, here we go then...

Battersea (*London*)

Brixton (*London*)

Bexhill (*Sussex*)

Bognor Regis (*Sussex*)

Folkestone (*Kent*)

Dover (*Kent*)

Carlisle (*Cumbria*)

Aberdeen (*Er?... Aberdeenshire*)

Killed a page, didn't it?

Newmarket (*Suffolk*),

Epsom (Surrey),

Lambourn (*Berkshire*)

And what is my TRUE favourite place in the UK?

That's right, Newcastle !!

I think I've lived in every corner of Britain, yet haven't lived in the one place I love the most. Still, at least not living there gives me the chance to visit more often. (Not that I would visit if I was living there, because that would just be fucking weird)

Well that was a short section, wasn't it? Wow, really scraping the barrel trying to find things to say now !!

Bugger

No, I'm not saying the word because I am struggling with the next part, I just really wanted to say the word,

Bugger

Say it yourself – Go on, try it,

Bugger

Very therapeutic, don't you think?

Go on, try it one last time, Call this part my audience participation.

Bugger

60+

Bugger

What? What was that "Bugger" for?

Oh, what was that (60+) for?

Nothing !!

Bugger

Just one of these questions, everyone seems to want to ask me – You know, after my slag-bag stint at Butlins and because of the sexual nature of my writing.

Bugger

Please, don't make me explain what 60+ means, or say it.

Bugger

Have you ever wondered what the word "Bugger" actually means? Bugger, a bit like bug, a bit like burger – Maybe it's a burger made out of bugs !!

Bugger

You got the question and answer yourself yet?

Can I move on?

60+

Bugger

Why the sixty plus?

Bugger, I thought you might ask that

Just looked up the word "Bugger" and here's the definition.

{Bugger is a slang word. The term is a general purpose expletive, used to imply dissatisfaction, or to refer to someone or something whose behaviour is in some way displeasing or perhaps surprising}

Bugger – Who fucking knew?

A bit like who fucking knows how many (**_60+_**) women there has been for me?

Slag – Sorry, I mean bugger

Bugger off, I lost count, okay

Hey, just reading over that definition, I guess I'm a "Bugger"

Bugger

I mean, you've paid for this book and all I've done for two minutes is say,

Bugger

I said you might call me a bugger, not want to

Bugger me

Which coincidentally, is what I actually thought,

Bugger meant

Bugger

So have you worked out the hidden confession I've been trying to answer for you?

Bugger

Are you satisfied you don't need to ask me that very personal question about my sex life now?

Bugger

No? Then, Fuck off

Bugger

CHAPTER 17
WINTER OR SUMMER

Right what next? What part of my life or personality haven't I shown yet? How about my favourite time of year?

My god, this is getting boringly tedious now, isn't it?

Bear with me !!

Am I a summer person or a winter person?

Go on, you have a guess first...

"Shit, I'm good at this audience participation thing, aren't I?"

Wow, are you getting to know me now? Did you answer (BOTH) like you knew I would answer? (Don't make me tell you to fuck off twice in the matter of seconds) Its both, okay?

Winter time is full of Christmas spirit, snow, freezing cold winds and joyfulness. It also the time of year I don't sweat like a monkeys arse and can cover my bald head up with a hat (Don't ask me where the monkeys arse came from – I haven't got a clue)

Summer is full off BBQ's, freshly cut grass, sexy flesh, skirts and a naked arse. (Hey, I'm a poet, who didn't know it)

Hold on...

Freezing cold winds, more clothes and the flu?

Sexy flesh, skirts and a naked arse?

"Can I change my mind as I am writing please?"

Summer time is my favourite time of the year, without a doubt !!

Wait, wait, wait...

Ew, then there's the fucking wasp. That pointless bastard that flies the fuck around and stings you on your naked sun-burnt nose.

Don't you just love it when you force yourself to stay calm in front of other people, then act all macho and shit, trying to shoo it away?

"I hate fucking wasps. Come near me and I will kill ya"

No, just me then, is it? Really?

Am I really the only knob that punches the air, misses every time, then karate kicks something like the table, screaming louder than I would being stung by the stripy fuck?

What I find even worse than the wasp threatening to turn your macho image into a whimpering child, is that one person that opens their mouth...

"Ooh, don't worry it's just a little wasp"

"Yeah, thanks for that Dorothy, I thought it was a fucking elephant"

"Just stand still, it won't hurt you"

Does anyone else have a problem with this kind of statement too, or is it just me again? Just stand still? It won't hurt you?

Er... Sorry love, but I happen to think standing still will actually give the bastard an easier target to fucking aim it.

What a crappy thing to say !!

"Oh bollocks, because of the dreaded wasp, I think I will change back to the winter after all"

Frosty mornings, log fires, snow...

(Oh shit, here comes the spider)

Why do the bastards always come into your house more when it's winter? I mean, I ain't thick or anything, I know they're cold, but why not piss off next door to the neighbours house? I don't think they're scared of the fuckers !!

How comes the biggest Twat on the planet, all fury legs and shit always scampers across my ceiling? And furthermore, always does it when there's something good on TV?

Oh dear, a little bit of a dilemma here – Spiders in the winter, wasps in the summer.

Why can't they come at the same time of year? Saying that, why can't the hairy spider eat all the fucking wasps, then get killed by the wasps sting as it enters it's hairy mouth?

(Job done, everyone's a winner)

I told you to bear with me, didn't I?

Fuck, it's not like I've EVER been asked this stupid question before – I mean, who comes up with this shit?

I know what, lets start again.

Ready?

"Jimmy, what do you prefer, winter or summer?"

"Rainbows !!"

CHAPTER 18
BIRTH

Well, I guess I am coming to the end of this book, considering I don't know what else you want to know about me and no-one is giving me a question to answer.

I did for your benefit, ask the wife what question I could cover next, but for some reason all I got was a...

"I wouldn't ask a question,

I know everything about you anyway"

(Dippy cow)

To further your reading, enjoyment or agony (However the case may be) I've decided to go back on my word and talk about my wonderful children. Well, when I say children, I mean the pregnancy part, the pain I suffered during it and the hardship that comes with being a man.

Oh fuck, this should be good !!

(All those "Girl Power" females, simply rip out the next few pages)

(Yeah, like right now)

(Stop fucking reading)

(I ain't carrying on until you've buggered off)

{WARNING}

For my own safety, please bear in mind that I am in no way, shape or form sexist - I write comedy for a living and shouldn't be attacked in the street if passed.

....

I don't know why (Because I know I'm only messing about) but I've kind of put myself off doing this part now.

"Deep breaths Jimmy, deep breaths"

*"Just take it slow, ease into it and **DON'T** offend anyone"*

Okay, I'm calm, relaxed here goes nothing...

Think you're the only gender, being female to go through the fucking pain?

Think it's all a walk in the park for us men?

Think we do nothing, but become non-supportive pricks?

Then fuck you !!

"Wow, that was easier than I thought it would be"

Well, where do I start?

I guess I better start by saying, just like my wedding day was a nightmare, pregnancy is up there with it too. Don't get me wrong, I love my kids more than anything in the world, but I would never go through that nine months of hell again. (And this is a bloke that's been through it four times)

Hey just think – Four times, nine months each – That means I've spent thirty-six months of my entire life living in pure hell.

(***Now you can do your fucking "ahhhhh" thing for me***)

No? Don't want to now? Fine !!

Now before I get started can I just say, I have the utmost respect for any woman that goes through pregnancy, the birthing procedure and I hold anyone in the highest regard for going through it all with a smile on their face.

Right here we go

My eldest son is called Jordan (Jordan James) born in 1999.

(Jordan because we never found out the sex, so wanted a modern unisex name) - (His second name is James, named after me Jimmy, which if you haven't already worked out thick-arse, is my real name)

Second in line was Justin (Justin George) born in 2004.

(Justin because we knew the baby was a boy, then because me and the wife were and still are Justin Timberlake fans) - (George was the name of my wonderful Grandfather and is also my middle name)

Next was another son Charlie (Charlie Zade) born in 2005.

Yes I know, very fast after Justin was born – What can I say? It was the wife's fault !!

(Charlie was simply a name we really liked, plus my uncle's name is Charlie too) - (Zade? Well, by this time we'd run out of boys names we liked, so when my parents were up visiting our newborn and the wife said she was thirsty, I picked up the Lucozade bottle and the decision was made)

"True story – One bottle of juice, one middle name !!"

My daughter called Georgia (Georgia Tamzin) born in 2007.

(Georgia again, for links to my grandfather's name) - (Tamzin after Tamzin Outhwaite, who is one of my favourite actresses)

And there you have it, my four beautiful children !!

So, where did the hell start?

Pretty much as soon as the pregnancy test was done and it was confirmed.

Okay, lets have a look what a woman goes through in a nut-shell – Feel feel to stop me if I get anything wrong, or misunderstand anything. Yeah, like you can in a bloody book !!

(Pee on a stick) - (Boobs start to get bigger) - (Morning sickness kicks in) - (The start of the weight gain) – (Cravings) -(More weight gain) - (Cramps, sweats, hot flushes, back ache)

"Did I miss anything above? Probably !!"

(Contractions) - (False alarm) - (More contractions) - (Labour)

"I think that's about it – I'm sure the wife will let me know if I've forgotten anything"

Okay, you ready for another shopping trip story, based on pregnancy?

You want to hear how I see things going?

...

"Jimmy I've just done a test and found out I'm pregnant"

"Er..."

"Er? Well don't sound too happy by the news, will you?"

Why does it seem every woman that tells a man she's pregnant for the first time, suddenly thinks he's going to break out into a merry dance or expect an instant happy response?

"I thought you would be happier?"

"Er..."

"You know, if you don't want a baby, you've only got to say"

"Er..."

Give the poor bloke time to adjust !!

Oh no, that's right, there's no time to adjust is there, because your breasts are hurting, your emotions are getting used to the news too and you're already dragging him down the hospital for the first scan.

"Look Jimmy, look on the ultrasound screen, it's our baby"

"Yeah I see"

"Look there's it's little hands, there's it's little feet"

Now is it just me, or am I the only fucker in the world that looks at one of these twelve week scan pictures and can't fucking see anything at all? In-fact I wouldn't say I can't see anything, because that would indicate I'm blind, but a smudge of something dark, then something really white looking, doesn't exactly say baby to me.

I bet somewhere in that ultrasound machine there's a little fucking printer, that is programmed to print off the same picture over and over again, because lets face it – Who has actually seen anything that looks any different to everyone else's scan?

"Ahhhhh look Jimmy, it's Tina and Mike's baby scan picture"

"No it's not, that looks exactly like one of mine"

"Don't be silly, it's Tina and Mike's baby... Sorry about him, he gets confused"

Oh do I? Do I really?

Hello Tina, nudge nudge, wink wink...

SORRY, GOT SIDETRACKED BY ANOTHER BOOK I AM CURRENTLY WORKING ON (Back to the story, where were we?)

Just done the scan, I'm dazed by the weird shapes on the ultrasound machine and...

...

Action !!

"Can you tell if it's a boy or girl?"

Thank fuck those nurses can't tell at this stage.

"Wouldn't you like to know the sex of our baby Jimmy?"

"Er..."

Come on nurse, time to say that magic line of yours...

"Sorry but it would only be a guess, it really is impossible to tell at this stage"

Thank fuck, I thought you'd never say it !!

How comes they say those same words every time? I mean, you'd think with medical science and the years that pass by, they'd at least improve their speech a little.

"I guess it's time we started talking names then?"

"Names?"

"Come on Jimmy, get with the programme, show some interest please"

"Interest?"

(I've just been told we're pregnant, I haven't got over the heart-attack shock yet and now you want me to start thinking names)

"I think it looks like a Gary, don't you?"

"Gary?"

"Yeah you know, on the scan picture?"

"Gary?"

"Ooh, what about Cindy?"

"Cindy?"

"Yeah, Gary if it's a boy, Cindy if it's a girl"

Er... How about we call it Bob, because it sounds like Blob and that's all that fucking scan picture is giving me right now.

"Come on, at least give me some names. Show a little bit of interest at least"

"Okay then, George"

"Neah, don't like it"

"Right, what about James?"

"Oh dear, oh no !!"

Oh no?

Oh no?

I happen to remember you saying "I do" to that same fucking name during our wedding, but it's an "Oh no" right now, is it?

Fuck this, I need a drink to settle my nerves !!

"What do you think you're doing?"

"Er?... Going down the pub for a drink"

"Oh no... No, no, No, no, NO !!"

I take it that's a no then?

"If I've got to give up having a drinking for nine months, then you've got to do the same. It's no good me giving up something I enjoy doing, if you're going to carry on doing it. We're supposed to be in this together, not me go through it alone, whilst you bugger off down the pub. Oh no, there's not going to be any drinking or any smoking for the next nine months, otherwise I won't be having this baby – Not with you anyway"

...

"Sorry, did you say something dear?"

...

Now, I'm a man of great restraint and can be very supportive, but I've had a heart-attack shock, been nagged about names and now she's demanding I give up everything I enjoy. Wow, loving this pregnancy thing so far... Ooh, I know what I am going to say...

"Okay love, if you're giving it all up, I will do the same"

I mean, why do we have to give up? We're not the one's that are pregnant. You wouldn't put a man through the snip, chop off his balls, then walk over to the wife and demand she slice off one of her nipples to even it out, would you?

No, that's right, you wouldn't...

"I can wait nine months for a drink, if it means making you happy baby"

Crossed fingers, jinx, padlock, touch wood.

Sorry, had to say all that, because if I don't have a drink in the next nine minutes, let alone nine months, I'm going to go insane !!

…

…

Hey look, I sneaked out of the house last night to have a quick one, meaning piss-up with the boys and she's doing the throwing up for me in the morning instead – Magic !!

Oh fucking no – Not magic – Not magic at all...

Here comes the hump, the grump and the lump all at once !!

"Ew, I feel terrible. Why do I feel so sick?"

Er... Because you're pregnant? Fuck me, even I knew that one...

"When will it be over?

When will this morning sickness go away?"

Well considering this is your first time being sick this morning, I'm guessing not very soon.

"Don't worry baby, It won't last long" I say rubbing her back, whilst her head is unattractively placed on the toilet seat and her hair is all stinky and knotted.

(So I've recently got over a massive shock, that I haven't been able to get over yet. I've been nagged about names, ordered to give up drinking and smoking, then watched her moan, feel sorry for herself and puke constantly for weeks)

Now come the cravings...

...

Bacon crisps, soaked in coffee...

crushed pickled egg, smeared in jam...

Oh how this reminds me of her period, the fucking period she isn't going to have now she's up the duff !!

I'm sure this part of pregnancy is some kind of karma, because whilst we stand around for those weeks watching her puke her guts out, we face this – Which coincidentally makes us want to puke our fucking guts up too, but no, we're not allowed, are we?

...

...

Finally the weight is gaining and it's time for the emotional bit.

"*I hate getting fat*"

"*Stop fucking eating so much then*"

"*Yeah but I'm eating for two now, aren't I?*"

Any excuse you fat cow !!

"*You don't find me attractive any more, do you?*"

"*Er...*"

"*You're going to leave me for someone younger, sexier and skinnier, aren't you?*"

Why, have you met her? Do you know her? Where does she live?

Emotion after emotion, I tell you, it's fucking exhausting work, all this listening !!

...

...

Finally the day is here, someone (Not me) pays her a compliment and tells her she's glowing. I think they actually meant growing, but got their words mixed up.

Guess what time it is now, yes it's shopping fucking time.

"Okay, we need nappies, we need formula, we need a car seat, we need a crib, we need loads and loads of baby clothes, we need bottles, we need baby monitors and we need some toys"

"Wow, got your list then? When did you make this out, when your head was half way down the toilet? Whilst you've been bitching at me for months? Or whilst you've been craving and eating your own egg and jam flavoured period?"

Tell you what I need (Something I never thought I'd hear myself say) I need some of those fucking *"Special Offers"* she loves so much, because this is going to cost a bomb !!

Oh no – No special offers when it comes to the baby. Everything in this section of life needs to be top of the range and the most expensive.

"Baby, sweetie, can I ask a question please?"

"YEAH, WHAT? IT BETTER BE SOMETHING GOOD"

Although glowing to others, still snapping at me, I see !!

"Why do I have to eat fooshty special offer cakes all the time, but the baby gets everything completely new and not past it's sell by date?"

The next speech that comes from her mouth is a monster – So big in-fact that it wouldn't be possible to fit into the book. So just in-case you're wondering, here's the much shorter version...

"You're scum, the babies not"

Okay, they weren't actually her words...

"The babies more important than you"

Yeah, that's the one !!

(So dodgy ticker now with all the shock and surprises at the start, nagged to death, moaned at constantly... Still haven't had a drink in months, watched her puke her face off, tried not to do the same during her horrid cravings, watched the person I once loved turn into a beached whale, then get told I'm not important any more – Oh and I've still only got my fooshty cake as reward for my efforts)

How are you feeling my emotional, beautifully pregnant wife? Because I am feeling down right drained, beaten up, tired, confused, unloved and a little hurt throughout all this so far...

Oh who am I kidding? I haven't had a proper shag in months now !!

Oh fuck, why did I have to mention sex?

"I'm not missing it, not missing it, honest"

Holy shit, here comes the horny beached whale...

"Really I'm fine, I'm so fine with not having sex in-fact, that I haven't masturbated since you fell pregnant – Please don't jump on top of me, please !!"

Yes it's that time of the pregnancy when a female gets incredibility horny and we have to muster up the courage to shag something so fucking fat.

"Tell me how much you love me"

"Tell me how much you want me"

"Tell me how much you still fancy me"

I would baby, but I'd be lying !!

How comes not only did our sex life disappear for a while, but now even the dirty talk has resorted to this? Wow, what I'd give for a...

"Tell me what a filthy whore I am" or *"Punish me for being a naughty girl"*

Nope, not a sausage – Coming out of her mouth, or in between my legs for that matter.

Nope, missionary isn't possible, can't climb on top of the bitch... And fuck no, she's not getting on top of me... Guess it's the old spoons position for us again. Hey, at least I don't have to look at her.

(So, dodgy ticker, nagged to death, moaned at constantly... Forgot what being drunk feels like, puke, holding back my puke, the beached whale, feeling unimportant, stuffing my face on fooshty *"Special offer"* cakes and now, I have to have sex with something I wouldn't even have sex with if I had my beer goggles on)

…

…

Ooh the end is in sight, she's finally having contractions. Wow, I hope these first little one's hurt the crap out of her – Call it payback for calling me unimportant.

(Back aches, headaches, sore feet) And that's just the start for me, as I go to work, rush home to be moaned at, visit all those dumb fucking pregnancy classes (Lets not go there) and race her backwards and forwards for hospital appointments.

Oh I see, **YOU'VE** got the back aches, headaches and sore feet, have you? Well excuse me for caring about my unloved self for a change. Ooh there's more is there?

(Hot flushes, feeling uncomfortable, sore nipples, sore hips, swollen joints) Hey, I only had really sore feet and you didn't give a shit about me, so why should I be bothered with your list of made-up pains?

…

The wait for those waters to break.

…

The wait for those REAL contractions to start.

…

118

Will the wait EVER fucking end?

...

...

Why is it, that when you're tired most, when you've exhausted every single part of your body and when you think you might be able to shut your eyes for just sixty seconds,

"Jimmy, my waters have broken"

FUCK !!

"Please don't be true, please let me have a little rest"

I'm not sure whether it's denial or the fact we're fucked by this stage, but why is it, even looking at the puddle of water on the floor, does our brain tell us it's something else?

"Are you sure they've broken?"

What a stupid fucking question !!

...

The panic, the rush to the hospital and here's another thing...

How comes in films you see this mad car crashing dash to the hospital, yet they never show that you didn't have to rush in the first place and you'd in-fact be sitting in that crappy hospital for hours on end?

...

Just when us men finally think we might get to sit down for a few minutes, this is where our reserve stamina kicks in... You see, whilst women constantly remind men that they don't go through the birthing process themselves, let me tell you, they do !!

Yes I know you push, I know you're tired and I know it hurts like buggery, but lets face the facts quickly... You're the one on the fucking bed, we're not... You're getting off your bloody nut on drugs, we're not... You're not the one facing the emotional battle ahead, we are...

"Mr Perrin, would you like to get your wife something to drink?"

"Mr Perrin, would you like to hold your wife's hand?"

"Mr Perrin, would you like to rub your wife's back?"

"Mr Perrin, would you like to do some breathing exercises with her?"

Yes, it's the bitch of a midwife, come to make our lives that little bit harder, whilst she talks to us like a child, orders us about, whilst you lay back happily and inhale those drugs.

"Mr Perrin, is this your first time?"

"Er, no... It's my third actually"

"Then why does it look like you have no idea what you're doing then?"

Hey, why doesn't someone just call old Mrs Steward in to shake me the fuck around and bring in the mother-in-law for good measure too, because I'm dying here !!

"Oh Mrs Perrin, how do you put up with him?"

"Men just aren't cut out for things like this, are they?"

Just you keep laughing at me bitch, because I'm about to kick you the fuck out of this room in a minute.

(Oh... Hold on... She's gone)

Why do these midwives come into the room, run your qualities and manhood down (Down so badly that you've lost every bit of confidence in yourself) then bugger off and leave you sitting there on your own until it's push time?

"Er... How about, come in, give me some confidence and then fuck off !!"

...

...

With all that confidence sailing away, your emotions over the last nine months catching up with you, or when that shock of actually being pregnant in the first place hits you, things then turn **REALLY** shitty. Yeah, it's okay for you sitting there drugged up to the eyeballs, but whilst us men sit there looking around the room at all the pipes, tubes and equipment, it's now we start to freak out inside.

What if something goes wrong?

What if a choice needs to be made between partner and baby?

The pressure really kicks in and it's one of the most scariest feelings in the world knowing we are your next of kin.

Not only are we emotionally drained and tired, but these fears are so strong, that all our love for our partner comes flooding back and we just want them to be okay. It's **HONESTLY** one of the loneliest places I've visited in my life and I've been back there four times.

...

Oh no – No time for "**Ahhhhh's**" right now,

we've got a baby to deliver.

Tiredness, wake up,

Emotions, piss off,

Time to be stronger than ever now !!

(Either that or faint on the floor like a pussy)

...

In rush the teams of doctors, in rushes that bitch of a midwife, then pushed out the way and forgotten about it's you. Nope, all you can do now is let your partner squeeze the fuck out of your hand, try and joke up the crazy experience as much as you can and PRAY !!

I Think during the whole nine months, the worst bit comes next. No, I don't mean when your baby is born, I mean when the midwife asks you if you want to hold your new baby.

Er... Well yeah I do, but I am so knackered.

"Your wife did so well Mr Perrin, that I think a good nights sleep and rest is in order now"

Really?

Really?

Really?

I mean, really?

What like I don't need a sleep too?

You don't want to cry because you're holding your newborn, you don't want to cry because everything went fine – You want to cry because none of the fuckers there think you need a rest too.

Oh no, it's a long drive home for you. Which is followed by six million phone calls to family and friends, then to check the house is ready for your newborn, before the race back over to the hospital first thing to pick the gang up.

(Where's my fucking sleep?)

HA, you thought that was the tough part for a man, didn't you?

WRONG !!

Well how about when you finally get back to the hospital, your newborn is wide awake and your partner looks amazing?

"Wow, you look really tired Jimmy,

didn't you sleep much last night?"

What, all of a sudden you care about me again, do you wife?

"So new daddy, are you ready for the endless nights of no sleep?"

Fuck off, Midwife bitch !!

Although this little story has plenty of real life experiences inside for me, I must say it wasn't as mental as this and during the four times I've experienced it, my wife has been nothing but perfectly amazing throughout. See, that's what makes her so special - She listens to the crap I've got to say (Serious or not) then always considers my feelings too.

The point to my story is – Yes it's mightily hard for a woman to jaunt through the nine emotional months of pregnancy, but it's no picnic for a man either. If you can take this journey together, then I guess you've got a marriage or relationship like mine.

CHAPTER 19
D.I.Y

Saying that about my marriage, things aren't always perfect between us. For instance, I could happily divorce the dippy cow when the decorating or some kind of D.I.Y needs to be done around the house – She drives me nuts !!

Here's how one of those conversations go at home

"*Jimmy, I think it's about time the ceiling had a lick of paint*"

"*Fair enough, I will get around to it*"

Now, when I say I will get around to doing it, it usually means at my very next available spare moment. Granted that might not be for a week or so, but my word is my word and I will do it.

What do I find when I go to start it a few weeks later? A quarter of the fucking ceiling already painted !!

"*I thought you wanted me to do this?*"

"*Yeah I did, but I knew you were busy, so decided to do it myself*"

"*And when are you planning to finish it then?*"

"*It'll get done*"

Those words will honestly be her famous last words, because

she's forever starting something and never finishing it. And when I say never, I mean **NEVER !!**

If there's one thing you'll learn about living with me, it's that I am incredibly fast. (Well, with everything except in the bedroom that is) When I say I will do a job, I get it done, there's no hanging about with me !!

Painted ceiling, double coat – Done, an hour...

Build a shed in the garden, from scratch – Done, an hour...

Put up the kids trampoline, single handedly – Done, ten minutes.

(I'm even like this with a book I'm writing)

Want the next in the Hard Up series? Want that book over three hundred pages long? - Done, four to six weeks. Nope, there's no six months to write a book with me (Like these other authors) everything needs to be done at a rapid pace and as fast as possible. Hey, why spend six days building a garden wall, when there's better things you could be doing? Wall? Simple, one day !!

Now ask me how I put up with my wife, or how she puts up with me, because we are so different when it comes to things like this. I mean, every single job I have to do around my house was done yesterday, yet there are still jobs she started something like six months ago, that haven't been finished yet.

I keep telling her, I'd rather decorate the whole house fast, enjoy it for a year, before having to repair or start again. Her way means taking a year to decorate the house, then as soon as you're finished one end, you start again the other.

When the fuck do you get time to enjoy the house finished? I'll tell you when,

NEVER !!

It's an ongoing battle with us and one that's been going on for twenty odd years. I think over the years I've taught myself there's no winning any more, so instead try to get everything done before she has a new bright idea and so far, so good, it's working that way. You know, I love to write, but sometimes wow, I hate fucking writing. See, whilst I sit here typing all this stuff down, she's out there somewhere... Somewhere out there stalking the house for something to do like a panther on the prowl – Creeping around looking for new projects to get started on, like a wildcat in search of it's next feed (Hey listen to me all intense and shit – Who says I can't write a gripping thriller one day?) Oh no, but not only is she looking for something to do but something she can do that means fucking avoiding all those jobs she's already started...

(Shhhh... Don't laugh, you might disturb it)

Okay I'd better get off this subject now, because I will either develop a nervous twitch or start freaking out so much, that I will force myself to stop writing and find out what she's up to now.

...

(Oh fuck it)

...

Yeah, just as I thought, she's currently measuring the staircase for a new project she wants to get started on (Told you) It's as though it's second nature to her, or second nature to me, knowing what comes next from the wildcat of a wife. Fuck it, didn't see anything, didn't hear anything, if I pretend I didn't just go out there, she might not actually get started.

(My god, ANOTHER bloody job I will have to finish off now)

Okay, before I do jump away from this subject and start talking about something else completely random, can I just say, although her "*Non-finishing job disease*" does my fucking nut in, I do hers in too. See, although I am fast and get things done a lot quicker, I've got my flaws too. With me and my lack of patience for fixing things, I usually lose it... In-fact I am REALLY good at this.

Gazebo threatening to fly away in the wind?

"*Jimmy, can you get your sexy butt out there and secure it?*"

"*Sure, no problem and thanks for noticing my pert derrière*"

That is honesty my attitude when asked to do something, well for at least five minutes anyway. That's before the peg holding the bastard gazebo in place bends out of shape and I get the hump. Before I know it, I am tearing the fucking thing down with my usual words,

"It's fucked, we'll buy a much better one"

It doesn't matter what it is, I am a sod for doing this.

"Jimmy can you fix the TV remote for the kids?"

"Sure, no problem and thanks for NOT noticing my pert bum today"

"I must have put some water weight on over night or something"

"Damn, what's her problem? No compliment? It's terrible"

"Talk about demoralising my get-up-and-go attitude"

"In-fact, I think I've got the right to sit here, refuse to fix it, until she says something nice"

…

…

…

…

"Hey gorgeous, I thought you were going to fix that remote?"

Finally, took your time, didn't you?

"On it now, not a problem"

Hey don't judge me... Some people need the magic word of please, I need some kind of compliment to get me motivated !!

As soon as that fucking remote refuses to let me fix it, it's in the bin. Oh no, but not only in the bin, but fucked worse than it was before I got my hands on it. Hey, I thought stamping on the son-of-a-bitch would make it work again.

*"**Fixed it yet Jimmy?**"*

"NOPE, it's knackered. We'll buy a much better one"

*"**Yeah but it only needed new batteries**"*

Yes, I am this bad... Oops !!

Saying that, why couldn't she stick some batteries in it herself? At least this way she could have felt good about actually getting something finished for a change.

And the mayhem of D-I-Y around the Perrin household goes on !!

CHAPTER 20
THE END PART

Well I guess that's **me**, the little book telling you about **me** as requested, yet not actually telling you much about **me** by the end of it (Or did it?) Well done, if you think you've got to know **me** better, then if you wouldn't mind, could you please tell **me**, who the fuck **me** is? Because I haven't got a fucking clue any more myself?

Some people call **me** crazy, some just think I'm got a wicked sense of humour, whatever you think of **me**, please don't judge **me.** Really and truthfully, all I live for is my family and those people that love **me** and I try to give double that love back as much as I possibly can – That's who **me** is !!

If you're wondering why I've highlighted the **me** words on this page, well that's because you wanted to read a book about **me,** so what better way to talk about **me**, than having a load of **me** words printed like this?

Call it my guilt

Because although I've told you more than I actually wanted to about **me**, I know it's not going to be the autobiography you expected to be reading.

*"Oh who am I kidding, it's just me trying to kill a few pages more, so this book about **me**, doesn't seem so fucking short"*

Before I go, let me just tell you were you can find **me** or get in touch with **me**. (Oh yeah, I can stop that **me** thing now, can't I?)

Firstly I have my very own website,

(WWW.JIMMYPERRIN.CO.UK)

It's run by one of my best friends Jenna and it's rubbish. Sorry Jen, don't mean that, I just hate seeing myself on the internet. No, really it's good... Nope, changed my mind again, it is In-fact rubbish.

I was just going to tell you how it displays my books wonderfully, has a few pictures of me on there and tells you a little bit about myself. BUT seeing as this book will do all that for you, what's the point in the fucking site? Sorry Jen, you're sacked !!

Yeah there is a page on there somewhere, where you can email me personally, but seeing as I don't check my email from week to week, it's not really that great either.

I guess I should also say that I am on Facebook, although I'm not actually on there !!

(WWW.FACEBOOK.COM/JIMMYPERRIN26)

I was ordered to join when I first started writing, but never actually use the thing.

"Hey Jimmy, why don't you join FB and promote your latest book?"

"Yeah, great idea !!"

People are as much interested in my release on there, like I am to hear what they cooked themselves for dinner last night, or which toothpaste they used to brush their teeth this morning. It really is the most shallow, self-centred "Give me fucking attention" - "Give me some sympathy" pile of crap I've ever experienced.

Don't get me wrong, it's a wonderful place to keep in touch with family and friends, but as for all the blogging and ego's, I just can't be bothered with it.

Tell a lie, the worst thing about it, is how so many people compete to have the most friends on there pages – Talk about the need to feel self-important. You have eight hundred and thirty-six friends, do you? Good for you, I would struggle to keep up with five on a daily basis, thanks very much... Saying that, I should turn around and confess I have over seven thousand followers on there and many celebrities linked to my friends list, shouldn't I? (Hey, now who is more self-important?) Yeah, like I'm going to have the time to talk to seven thousand people - I struggle to hold a conversation with people I've known for years, let alone people I don't even know.

(Twitter)

Fuck no !!

I'd rather cum in my own mouth, than use that waste of time website. Why do you think I love badminton so much? Because I think about the blue little tweeting bird thing and whack the shit out of it...

(Wow, I love all this freedom of speech stuff in this country)

Just as well really, isn't it?

As well as many book selling websites out there, my own site and WH Smith who stock my books on their system (Too rude for the shelves) Amazon also sell my books.

(WWW.AMAZON.CO.UK)

or

(AMAZON.COM)

or

(AMAZON.DE)

In-fact just type Amazon, followed by Jimmy Perrin and whatever country you're living in, you'll find me somewhere.

Finally I'm also a good-reads author on Goodreads.

(WWW.GOODREADS.COM)

In-fact this is the one site on the internet that I actually enjoy being on. Don't get me wrong, I don't really have the time to log-in on there either, but it is less for people blogging about the new wallpaper in their living room and more about people that read.

Unlike my email account and FB message button thingy, I *DO* happen to answer users questions on this site and *DO* plan to visit the site more in the future.

Saying that, I've just logged in on there to say hello to a few people, as I am writing this and found out something I'm not that happy about...

My official rating as an author on the site is currently **4.33**

"That's out of five you knob-head, not ten"

"Wow, do you really think my writing is that crap?"

Not bad, is it? Yeah, I guess it's something to smile about and be proud of. Hold on a god damn fucking minute...

Then I took a look at the individual ratings for my first three books.

Hard Up, Ardon 1, sits at **4.38**

Hard Up, Ardon 2, sits at **4.60**

And...

Heavenly Harold's Hell, sits at **3.75**

How the fuck is both Hard Up's rated higher than me?

"I know people call me over sensitive, but fuck me"

Does this mean the books I write are better than me?

How does it work, if I write the fucking things?

Clearly there's something wrong here !!

I mean, does that mean Malcolm and Dexter are more popular than me?

Do people really love them more than me?

BASTARD'S !!

Remember me telling you that I write the plot-line for the books in advance and the fact I am working on Hard Up 4, before I've released number three? Well, fuck that – Back to the plot-lines for me this afternoon, lets see how you feel about me when I kill one of those characters off, that you like better than me.

"Up my personal rating on Goodreads people, or Malcolm and Dexter get it !!"

So as you can see by reading about the websites I'm on, there's not really any chance of you communicating with me really, is there? Hey, that's how I like it – After all, I do have writing to do !!

Please don't misunderstand me as I finish off this book for you, because I am in no way unapproachable. I just spend a lot of my free time (When I get some free time) with people I love.

I tell you what – To prove I'm not unapproachable in any way, shape or form, I'm going to do something completely nuts (Yeah, imagine that, me doing something crazy)

Forget emails, leaving me messages on social websites, or anything else you do to try and get me to pick up my phone,

Text me !!

See, I might be really bad at answering messages, getting back to people or especially phone calls, but I don't mind the odd text now and again, then furthermore, I usually answer them.

Text me, go on, let me show you I can say hello back.

You haven't got my mobile number, have you?

Here comes the crazy bit then...

0790776707#

"Wow, you didn't actually think I would type in my full number, did you?"

Nope, one number missing, one number to find.

Fuck, if you do take the time to work it out, then I guess you are worth talking too !!

Saying that, what's so crazy about me doing this? If it gets too much, if I get bombarded with text messages, I can simply change my number, can't I?

I REALLY do hope you've enjoyed reading this little book about me and I DO hope it's made you smile. Although it's been said some of my readers want to get to know me a little more, my real reason for this book was simple... It goes right back to the beginning, where I told everyone I'm not a stand-up comic, just because I write comedy, so here's me doing it in a book instead

"Stand-up, sitting down"

If I've made you smile a little, thank you.

(Try harder to laugh next time you tit)

If I've made you laugh, let me know.

(Remember, that's all the motivation I need to keep me writing this kind of book for you)

If you haven't smiled or laughed... Shall I say it?

"No I won't... Thanks for giving me a try anyway"

Saying that you miserable arse-bag, I don't care
– I've already been paid for your purchase, so I'm
laughing for you !!

Wow, writing pretty much finished and now it's time to see the final cover they've designed for me... Bear with me...

…

…

"...???..."

…

…

Sorry, that above was me pretending to be speechless for a while.

So they went with the four of me and my backside then, I see...

Am I happy with the cover?

"Yeah, but no"

I mean, I guess it looks okay, but seeing as I don't like attention or my photo taken anyway, an okay from me at this moment in time means I'm pretty ecstatic about it.

Hey, at least they didn't go with the full-frontal one of me in my pants, because that was a picture !!

The wife said I looked like a porn-star and I must admit, I was actually impressed with my bulging package myself.

Saying that, sensitive me coming back now...

"Why didn't they use that picture? Why would they prefer to see the back of me?"

Saying that and then that again, how does it feel being a woman now asking that famous question,

"*Does my bum look big in these?*"

Try being me...

"Does my bum look big on my book cover?"

Wow, my eagerness for this book to be released has suddenly disappeared rather fast !!

I Hope you've enjoyed yourself – I hope you had a laugh with me, or at my expense at least.

Hope you'll be reading another one of my books real soon.

(God bless)

Jimmy

xx

OTHER JIMMY BOOKS

Hard Up, Ardon 1 (ISBN) 978-1492887041
Hard Up, Ardon 2 (ISBN) 978-1492888482
Heavenly Harold's Hell (ISBN) 978-1492890157
Air Hostess (ISBN) 978-1494423667

COMING NEXT

Hard Up, Ardon 3 – Due Summer '2014

"Here we go once more as Malcolm and the gang are ready to do battle with their chaotic lifestyles and unpredictable behaviours for the third time...
With Dexter now ready to start his new fireman career with Mike, the guy who openly had an affair with his wife Becky, then Malcolm jetting off on holiday with girlfriend Sally, planning to marry her and have an overseas wedding, it all sounds rather straight forward...
Straight forward? Dexter holding a fire hose? A stag night to attend? A wedding to reach on time? And a new girl called Candy rocking the boat? Surely things aren't going to get all crazy again"

WWW.JIMMYPERRIN.CO.UK

Printed in Great Britain
by Amazon.co.uk, Ltd.,
Marston Gate.